Submission.

Rules and Principles of Submission Grappling.

Nigel. S. J. Law

DEDICATION

To my wife Jane, and Richard and Nancy, my son and daughter.

CONTENTS

ACKNOWLEDGMENTS

Thanks are required to the following martial artists;

Andy Steele
Ken Erickson
Gary Savage

1 INTRODUCTION:

Having run a martial arts club and met many, many people interested in learning how to fight I realise what the ancient martial artists discovered. A code, honour, manners, discipline; what is referred to as a way, is very important. It is a sacred thing to train with someone, to put yourself in a vulnerable position, to have them vulnerable to you. All to learn and to teach how to fight.

It is a dichotomy that it is referred to as an art yet it is fighting, which, particularly too many modern sensibilities, is a form of barbarism. But there will always be the fight. Life can be cruel and all life is suffering and it is best to be as prepared as you can be.

Martial arts are often referred to as a journey of discovery. If your journey is easy you will learn little. If you are suffering, then open your mind and learn. Over the following pages I will tell you all I know about martial arts. I will be as true I can be and maybe you will find something of use to you.

If you are looking for individual techniques there are many books and of course there is everything you could wish for on the internet. For my little piece I want to talk about the other stuff, the thinking behind the techniques, the strategies and principles. I have written a series of paragraphs in such a way as to spur your imagination and your visualisation. I would like each paragraph to be read with an open mind, for you to look for recognition of the same situation, for similar situations or for other related contexts in which they can be applied.

Before then, a little history. I have not really followed the martial art scene. I do not watch many fights. I do not slavishly follow the fighters. This is from personal experience, not from second hand. This is all from those people who I have fought, what I have done to them and what they have done and tried to do to me.

I had done Ju-Jitsu from seventeen to nineteen. I was young, small at five feet five, five feet six maybe on a good day and I tried to keep out of the limelight. It was good tough training and I got tougher. Then I left my home town for university. Over the years I would occasionally think of going back to martial arts. I tried Karate. Maybe it was just that club but I found it unrealistic and weak and dropped out. Suddenly I was thirty five and worried about being unfit and went to try Judo. The Judo class had folded but I came across a newly starting club in something called Brazilian Ju-Jitsu with an enigmatic and inspiring instructor.

Brazilian Ju-Jitsu, and the Gracie family exploded onto the martial arts scene and the tentacles of it spread throughout the world reaching even my small little North of England town. It was a breakthrough, like the invention of computers. Where there had been nothing before there was an avalanche of new moves, new discoveries, and people making their names. People came through the door from far and wide who had done boxing, karate, ju-jitsu, judo all hailing this new martial art as the real thing, a mixed martial art, taking the best of everything. It was an incredibly rich and vibrant learning atmosphere. I have never learned anything so quickly and in one sense, so easily. A person who had been with us a few months would beat someone who had trained at other clubs for a decade. In another sense it was hard trying to keep up with it all.

Then two things happened that would set the pathway forward. One night I was lay in bed and I was brooding over being tapped out to an arm bar. I was running through it in my mind. I could see the technical mistakes I had made but there was something bothering me. I then had a weird conversation with myself about my own arrogance about not wanting to lose. Then I made a very clear and calm decision. A voice said, 'No, it is not arrogant to never want to lose, it is the purest true way to fight.' I said to myself, 'Of course I might lose but I will always try my best to win.' I then had the strangest feeling run through my body from my core out to my fingertips, down to my toes and up to my head as if I was unfolding and coming to my full height.

The second thing that happened around the same time was that my enigmatic and inspiring instructor who had taken me on as his number two, referring to his wandering half Gypsy blood upped and left for a new town. I was now running a fighting martial arts club where anyone could come through the door and lay down a challenge. If you are running a fighting martial arts club then you really cannot lose. You have to win to be in charge and, more than that, you have to be the big dog. You have to be the discipline that keeps everyone in line, everyone safe.

For the next four years I ran this open mat fighting martial arts club. The style could best be described as submission grappling. Sometime over those years I realised that, ever since my decision, I had remained unbeaten. This was thousands of fights with hundreds of people.

Indeed I could not say why I won. I knew there were people who could beat me, I just never fought anyone who did. When I came off the mat at the end of a session exhausted and looked around I would see people taller, heavier, fitter, stronger, some older, some younger; people far more experienced than me, people who followed all the fighters, read all the books, watched all the training programs. I had some epic fights and some that could have gone either way but for whatever reason I won them all.

2 SUBMISSION GRAPPLING RULES

Two opponents face each other from their knees or with one foot up. They slap hands and then fight to the following rules. You may start the same way from standing but this massively increases the chance of injury as one person tries to take the other to the floor.

POSITIVES.
Fix the position of your opponent and then hyper-extend a joint or other finish by following the A→B→C Rule.
A → The start of your move.
B → Give your opponent the opportunity and the time to tap out which is the signal that they quit.
C → Is when the move would finish with a break or damage to your opponent if it was for real.

Some moves require more care than others such as chokes, strangles, neck cranks, bending fingers, particularly the little finger. You may decide to stop a move if you sense that your opponent is being naive or even stupid with their own safety and explain why you stopped.

(If they do not believe you and say that they were fine or they thought you were only doing it because you were scared to lose, then inform your instructor. This is rare and it maybe that they are extremely arrogant or a stupid person).

The following don'ts are because they go straight from A to C inflicting damage without your opponent having an opportunity to submit. Of course they are available in a real fight.

DON'T'S.
No striking (punching, kicking, kneeing, elbows, head butts, chins etc).
No scratching.
No biting.
No pulling hair.
No gouging.

In other words you do not twist your opponent's arm so hard and fast they do not have the opportunity to quit before it breaks, or you do not throw your opponent about in such a way as to not know how they will fall or twist and cause them injury through such carelessness.

You are taking your body to an extreme in a physical competition that is similar to chess with move, counter move, counter counter move etc, but should come off the mat with body in one piece.

You fight each other for basic hold down positions from which you try to force your opponent to tap out.

You do not wear traditional martial arts gis if you do not want to. You are not an Asian peasant from the sixteen hundreds. You do not need to grade belts. You do not need to bow. You do need to show each other respect, tap hands as a signal you are both ready. You grapple until one person submits. If you win you win, if you lose you lose, and that is it.

3 SUBMISSION GRAPPLING STRUCTURE

You can look on submission grappling as a system of fighting and think that strength will always win but it is also a lot like chess in that there can be set moves, counter moves, counter counter moves.

There are four main basic elements.

1.   Dominant positions or hold downs.
2.   Transitions (including reversals).
3.   Escapes.
4.   Submissions

You can visualise all the moves in a big map radiating out from each of the basic hold down positions. If your opponent tries a particular escape, you counter and then he follows. If you have a particular position you can attempt a submission, which he then defends. You can learn the defence for yourself and then come up with a move to beat that and so and so on. In this way your knowledge and the internal map of it expands out.

This map is developing all the time. A particular move may be devastating or successful for quite some time and then a way is found to counter it and its importance subsides and then something else becomes dominant.

Much of the map, or the way of fighting is haphazard until some one good at something lays out their successful method and fills in the gaps for everyone and then it is added to and adapted.

It is a beautiful thing.

4 STRATEGY

1.   Basics.
2.   The start.
3.   Set traps.
4.   Sit and wait.
5.   Position before submission.
6.   Defence and attack.
7.   Sacrifice.
8.   Awareness.
9.   Analyse losses and errors.
10.   Constant attack.
11.   Hold downs.
12.   Pretend – to break the stalemate.
13.   Hesitation.
14.   Personalities.
15.   The transition.
16.   Elegance.
17.   Fight off centre.

STRATEGY.

∞‡∞
Basics.

All things being equal, stick to your basics and crush your opponent.

Although you should know as many finishes as possible and look for them in every possible position in every possible way, eighty percent of your finishes will be your basics and you should become a master of them.

∞‡∞
The start.

Fight strongly at the start to gain the dominant position. Do not give up a dominant position to your opponent to save energy and tell yourself you will fight hard from there. It will be worse from there, fight now. Tell yourself your opponent is suffering more than you. Tell yourself you can rest a little when you have achieved a dominant position. You will be surprised to find hidden strength and how a seemingly strong opponent can suddenly give way.

The only time you should go against this is for those very strong opponents who you know will eventually tire you and take a dominant position. In these cases you must not fight until you tire because you will lose. You must conserve your energy and if your opponent is eventually going to force you over, induce him to do so at your advantage, for example by pulling him into your guard.

∞‡∞
Set traps.

This can be a very successful strategy. There is nothing like setting a trap. While it is great to be fluid and have no set strategy, that will be the case when you are fighting well and, let's be honest, beating someone you are likely going to beat anyway. Traps are invaluable in close fights, when you are tired, when your opponent is stronger than you. When you are at some form of disadvantage. They are invaluable, in that, because you know before hand what is going to happen, and your opponent does not, you are much more likely to make it happen and work.

It is like the breaking test in your driving test. They say to add on reaction time to the breaking time. You are taking away that time. Also, let's say for example, you are trying to trap an arm for a lock. There will be an optimal position you would like your opponent's arm to be in so that you have the greatest chance of success. In setting a trap you can time your move to trap his arm in that best position. In not knowing beforehand your timing could be slightly out, you snatch at your opportunity and the opponent's arm has gone past the optimum position and they can fight to release it.

Great fighters often talk about having no set plan and that is fine for them, but us mere mortals often have to have some sort of plan.

∞‡∞
Sit and wait.

You will find it a very productive strategy to sit and wait for your opponent to make the first move. If you are in a dominant position you will not have to make the first move. If you are not in a dominant position and nothing is happening to you, again, you do not have to make the first move. When someone moves it gives opportunities to you.

∞‡∞
Position before submission.

You will find it near impossible to finish your opponent without first gaining control of him with a good position. It is probably the foundation principle, position before submission.

∞‡∞
Defence and attack.

New fighters only think of attack and blunder directly into defeat. Defence is less glamorous than attack and is often neglected. The clever fighter soon learns how important defence is because you will first have to learn how not to lose before you can learn how to win.

All great fighters have a good defence. Remember this and do not neglect it.

∞‡∞
Sacrifice.

The use of sacrifice can be very advantageous. You may sacrifice position. This is usually against an opponent coming forward. Instead of trying to force him back, let yourself fall back and either take a submission or a position that suits you, or perhaps use his momentum to reverse him.

You may also sacrifice in a different way, for example, your opponent could be attacking your chin with his forearm. Instead of defending your chin, you may let him crush you down, drawing him forward, letting him think he is about to win. He becomes exposed without knowing. You spring your legs up to take an arm bar on the arm that was attacking you.

You may sacrifice a little to gain a lot. For example, your opponent may have you in his guard with his legs wrapped around your waist and is making it very difficult for you, attacking you with his arms and crushing you with his legs so that you have to sit very low and hold him around his waist. What you do is let your arm come a little away from your body. This tempts him to reach over and wrap it up with both his arms to try for a finish, but you have hold of your clothing and you know before hand you will be able to resist him. As he attempts the finish you lead him on by letting your arm move a little to encourage him to release his grip around your waist with his legs. When his legs release you, which is what you wanted, you hop over his leg and take a favourable position for you. He may still hold your arm but it is now useless to him because you have the dominant position. He realises his mistake, knows he cannot finish you and has to let you go.

∞‡∞
Awareness.

Awareness is the key thing in a fight. In all the confusion and the pressure of the situation if you can remain aware you will be the one to see the opportunities that arise. This is strongly linked to letting go and to creating pressure. Letting go means that you let go physical and mentally of things that are not important. Creating pressure means to cause your opponent to be occupied with seemingly important things. It is not just about thinking clearly, this is very difficult in the confusion of a fight, it is about thinking more clearly than your opponent.

You need to develop three eyes, two consciousness's or to split your consciousness into different percentages. Your concentration varies in percentages. It is like cooking a big many course meal and you have lots of preparation, lots of pans to watch at the same time. When it is going well you have a sense of control over the whole thing and you are able to listen to his breathing, follow his movements, think ahead on his moves and yours, looking for weaknesses and opportunities. You know where each part of his body is, particularly his arms, hips and neck. At times you have to put most, if not all, your attention onto one thing, for example if he launches a powerful attack and you have to give everything to defend it. Or if you are in the final part of trying to put him into a position and he is desperately defending it and you have to fully concentrate. You are particularly looking for changes, something unexpected might catch more of your attention, such as if he put his hand in an unexpected place and you have to evaluate his intentions. Is it a move? Is it a mistake? Is it a trap? Is it just to distract you?

The time to bring your focus together most is for your attacks. These are key to your success and often require great strength combined with minute accuracy of movement.

Another way is to have moves like fire and forget missiles. For example, you are on top of your opponent in side control and he is comfortable and giving you no opportunity to find a finish. You tell your shoulder to crush into his head but after you send the message you drain your attention away from it and wait for his arm to come out of its hiding place. If you remain concentrating on your shoulder you will miss the opportunity of his arm.

∞✝∞
Analyse loses and errors.

Good fighters think far more of their losses than they do of their wins. They analyse them to try to eradicate them. To be able to do that you must be able to trace the origin of your error, because there will be an error. If they caught your arm, when did they first go to wrap up your arm? Before that, how did they entice you into a position where it was possible for them to go for your arm? Before that, how could it be possible for them to have gained the dominant position from where they were able to entice you? Before that how come they were able to tip your balance to gain their position? Before that, how come they were able to control the speed and rhythm of the fight? You may find your lose started a long way from the final moment.

Often it is good to ask your opponent to explain to you how they were able to beat you. They will probably tell you something simple and obvious that you may have missed. They may give you good advice, sometimes without meaning to. "Yes, and I almost gave up on it". "You could have easily reversed me". "I only went for it because I was so tired". "You gave me the idea when you put your arm there". These comments can be invaluable.

∞‡∞
Constant attack.

Whatever position you are in you should always consider and at least be waiting to attack. There is nothing more demoralising for an opponent than to save himself from your attack and then to be faced with another and then another.

Quite often your opponent will give up at this point by, for example, letting you take his arm. He will pretend he didn't give up but you should know the difference and never let yourself be caught acting in such a way. You should only be beaten when you are beaten.

∞‡∞
Hold downs.

The first use of a hold down position is to stop your opponent beating you. This maybe sufficient to your situation in training, competition or a real fight. In some competitions you will get points for this but really this is only a draw, not a win.

The second aim of your hold down is to force a submission. If there is no pressure from your hold down your opponent can sit and wait you out. Your hold down should create such pressure that if he does not try to escape he will suffer greatly. Make him feel the longer he leaves it the weaker he will be and the bigger and wilder movement he will have to make to escape. You need to make him feel he is heading towards submission. Put pressure on his lungs with your weight, force your shoulder into his jaw, lift his head towards his chest or something similar to create this pressure so that he is forced to leave his defensive position.

∞‡∞
Pretend – To break the stalemate.

There are many forms of fakery and disguise and this is one specific instance.

You will find you will use the following strategy most often when nothing is happening and you are in stalemate. You should pretend to be trying to get something, for example his arm or his neck. You should make a great fuss of it and act like you are searching fiercely. Pretend that you know what you are doing and that your attack will have success soon. Often this convinces your opponent that you are onto something and he moves position breaking the stalemate in your favour. He will often gladly give a beneficial position to you thinking that he is happy to have successfully defended the attack which of course did not exist.

∞‡∞
Hesitation.

Sometimes your opponent will give away that he is unsure what to do, for example, he may have gained a top hold down and then switch between a number of positions, obviously unsure. This will be most likely backwards and forwards between two positions. If he does this, then wait for him to start to move positions and move yourself decisively and forcefully. You are moving at the maximum point of his confusion. His mind will become even more confused and perhaps even panic at your certainty. You will be able to take advantage and he will not know he was the author of his own downfall.

We all have the feeling that time can move at different speeds depending on how stressful the situation is. This is an example of that. He will feel, due to his stress and confusion, that you have leapt through time to get him.

Conversely you may at times act confused, switching about without apparent reason, while waiting for your opponent to come out of his defensive position in a false sense of safety.

∞‡∞
Personalities.

Experienced fighters can develop strategies without realising it based on, for want of a better word, their personalities. One is offensive based, one defensive based. You can also think of them as one open, one closed. When you become aware of your style, often when you come across someone very good of the opposite style, you will need to make an effort not to be put off your game.

There have been many famous clashes of this nature in fighting and in sport in general. Often one party becomes frustrated at the clash of styles, frustrated that they can not operate as they want and have been used to. Sometimes they have become so frustrated that they have given up, even when they have more to give. Sometimes they have become so enamoured at the difference and the shock of defeat they have attempted to change their entire style, or even so humiliated they have quit suddenly and entirely.

While it is okay to experiment with the opposite style and learn from it, you should not chop and change between the two to the point that you become confused, forget who you are and have no base strategy.

It is an oft stated truth that you should always be learning. It is equally a truth that there are some things about you that you should never change.

∞‡∞
The Transition.

You can look at submission grappling as a series of moves and counter moves. A series of positions to fight for and from those positions submissions to be gained. The next step up from that is mastery of the transition. Being aware of not just the end position you are aiming for but the path in between.

While opponents are fighting to gain one of the set positions they should become more and more aware of these transient positions as positions themselves. The gaps between moves fill in with knowledge and can be fought over themselves. Why let your opponent settle into a position and then try your escape just because you have practiced it from there. Fight constantly all the time, every inch of the way. Fight in the transition as well as the position until the two become blurred. This kind of fighting is difficult to cope with. No fixed position in mind, one continuity, every position equally as good as any other. It is trying to meet flow from another direction.

However, a person who is fighting in this way when they first learn it will probably fight at one steady speed through out because of the energy required. A good fighter can counter this with changes of speed.

∞‡∞
Elegance.

Often a fighter can become obsessed with positions and moving between them. This must be remembered as a partial objective, the full object is to win by submission. A fighter can blind himself with fancy movements that achieve nothing and a less elegant fighter who is more directed, catches them with a finish. The person who lost must analyse this thoroughly as they may fall into the trap of thinking they have to be even more elegant and more complex and miss the reason for their loss.

A fighter should know what positions lead to what finishes and when they have obtained their position they should immediately seek the submission. It is criminal for a fighter to fight to gain a position and then leave it for something else without making use of that position to try to beat or weaken their opponent. In moving from one secure position to another you give opportunities and relief to your opponent.

∞‡∞
Fight off centre or Asymmetry.

A fight is won when strength overcomes weakness. What does it matter if your opponent is stronger than you, or fitter or faster or taller? You do not have to be stronger than him everywhere, just in one place. Everyone is quickly aware of this.

You can over power by numbers such as two arms attacking one. You can over power by strong attacking weak such as arms attacking neck. You are not winning by symmetry you are over powering with asymmetry.

Another more complex form of this is fighting, having your weight, off centre from him. This again is asymmetrical. It means that your power, in relation to him, is not split fifty fifty either way but has a dominant part and weak part. In this type of fighting you must attack or defend with the dominant part and keep the weak part from him.

A simple analogy of this is in football. If the opposition has the ball and its players are spread out you may send four or five players to crowd and get the ball from the opposition who have two players near the ball. You will have more numbers where the ball is and are likely to win it back. The opposition will have spare players somewhere else on the pitch but if they are far away from the ball, what does it matter because they have no influence. Even if the opposition manage to keep the ball and pass it towards the free player, by the time the ball has arrived the players can move over so he is no longer free.

This is not something that is easy and does not come naturally to beginners so will come later in your development. Fighting off centre gives you what is called in physics, potential.

5 TACTICS

1. The neck.
2. Relieving pressure.
3. Strength 1.
4. Strength 2.
5. Pressure.
6. Rhythm/Tempo.
7. Chasing the arm.
8. Do not give him what he wants.
9. Give him what he wants.
10. Arms and legs, shoulders and hips, centres.
11. Listen to what your opponent says.
12. Float.
13. Riding.
14. Mimic.
15. Distance.
16. Centres.
17. Indecision.
18. Put your hand over his face.
19. Assessment.
20. Destroy his base/position.
21. Align him.

TACTICS.

The neck.

In sport there are go to players. Players who the team turn to when they are under pressure to rescue them. You should look on your opponent's neck as one of the main go to places if you are under pressure.

The neck is a major weak point in your opponent. It is a prime target, particularly in an opponent with exceptional strength in his arms and legs. As part of your radar you must try to be aware of the position of your opponent's neck at all times. If your opponent makes a sudden very strong and effective attack it may be possible to stop it by not stopping his actual attack but by directly and strongly attacking his neck.

You can often use this as a defence against someone who turns their back to you and attacks your legs for a leg lock. Rather than trying to directly free your legs, pull your opponent very forcefully back towards you with the blade of your wrist into their neck. Leg locks are very clumsy and dangerous. You may be quite savage in your attack on his neck, obviously not to the point of danger, but enough to convince him not to attempt leg locks again against you.

Leg locks are dangerous. When someone puts a leg lock on you may feel secure but it is in their nature for the leg muscles to suddenly give way on this type of attack. Your opponent will know this. He will also know that it is somewhat of a desperate attack as going for leg locks leaves him wide open to a counter attack and he should not be shocked that you treat him strongly.

∞✝∞
Relieving pressure.

If you find yourself under a lot of pressure you will need to relieve this. Here is how you can do this.

There may be a specific defence technique that blocks that attack and you just need to learn and perfect that.

By a slight movement. Often all is required is a slight altering of a position and an unbearable attack becomes bearable. If you have time, try it.

Turn the tables. Can you launch an attack, even a pretend one, so that your opponent forgets about his attack? If your attack is not successful or it is a pretend attack you must use it to change your position so that the previous attack can not be launched, unless you can relieve it in the same way as before.

A big movement. This can be a desperate move because it uses up so much strength and if your opponent is clever it will signal to him that you are desperate and that if he fights hard he may soon have a victory. If you escape your position you must quickly secure an advantageous one. If you do your opponent may be disheartened at losing his dominant position. If he takes advantage of your temporary weakness and reverses you again, you must not be disheartened.

Coasters. Coasters under the wheels of furniture stop deep grooves being cut in carpets and floors. You can use this principle in the following way. You can relieve pressure, for example, from your opponents elbow pressing down into you, by placing your hand underneath it. Be careful that your opponent is not waiting for you to do this and setting you up in a trap. A version of this is scrunching your body. You are making bigger the area of your body that is in contact with the attack point so spreading the pressure. It will also be bringing more resistant muscles into play.

Deflection. You might not be able to push off an attack point or move away from it, but if you can turn your body the attack point could be partially deflected off.

∞‡∞
Strength 1.

Strength in one sense is very simple and can be looked at as a quantity. One fighter might have so much of it and another fighter has more and it will be obvious to every body. However, in that simplicity there can be built a great deal of complex variations.

Firstly, strength is relative. A person may be the strongest in your club for a number of years and then a monster of a fighter walks through the door and their whole approach has to change. Someone who has been relatively weak may have the opposite situation. Someone weaker than them arrives and they will be confused and strangely disappointed when they do not know what to do with their easy victories.

Strength will always be an attribute and is one of the major deciders in victories. The strongest are always amongst the top fighters at a club, however, the strongest is often not the best fighter. The strongest have their very strength an impediment to their progress. They have too many easy victories that they learn nothing from. They can escape from many attacks that they blindly walk into because of their strength.

As an instructor you have to try to get your strong fighters to fight as if they are not strong as part of their training. Many strong fighters find this almost impossible because they do not believe the truth of it. This is why they often remain behind someone not as strong as them who they cannot beat. They will not take one step back to take the two steps forward.

The best thing for strong fighters is for them to fight people as strong as them and then they can concentrate more on their technique. If you do not have any available then the weaker members are often good to train with. The excessively strong person will completely relax and just go for technique with them.

If you have someone who is exceptionally strong it can be a burden on your club. Many of the weaker fighters will become quickly disheartened and not want to fight them, but they ensure that the club does not stall in its progress and everyone has to up their game. Hold downs and finishes have to be that little bit more perfect to be able to cope. If you look on people like that as a challenge and try your best you will improve.

∞‡∞
Strength 2.

If your opponent is stronger, bigger, more fit than you, you may find it necessary to tire him before you try to finish him. It is like the deep sea fisherman and how they catch the big fish. How you do this is in the following ways:-

Make him move. If you can keep him on the move, making him travel more than you this will tire him quicker than you. If he is heavier than you he will tire quicker than you if you travel the same distance because he is having to move his heavier weight. If he is a lot heavier than you then you may even make him tired moving less than you. Some people are so big and heavy, even if they look quite fit, that they have an intense dislike of moving. They quickly become frustrated, stop moving and launch an attack. They may even succumb to a poor position just to be able to stop moving. You may decide to forgo this offered position, keep moving and make them more tired and frustrated before engaging. You can make him move by encouraging him to believe he is about to gain something, such as a hold down, but at the last moment you mysteriously manage to avoid it. You hold out the bait again and make him chase it again.

Make him move you. For example if you have a hold down and he tries to lift you and your main resistance to this is your weight, he is putting the energy in to move you and you are not putting the same energy in. If you finish in the same hold down position as before you now have a better position because it is the same position as before but now your opponent has less energy. You can make him move you to cause him to lose strength and energy by, for example, having him in a good hold down and then pressing the point of your elbow into his jaw line and leaning your weight into him. To stop your attack which is costing you very little energy he may lift your weight up off his which costs him a lot of energy.

Make him power up. If you jog a hundred metres you will lose far less energy than if you sprint a hundred metres, even though it is the same distance. If you sprint at your maximum fastest speed you will burn through all your energy and temporarily have no energy at all, you will be struggling to even breathe. Burning power is not a linear relationship, it is a to the power relationship. In other words, if you want to double the strength you will need to put in something like four times the power, not double. If you can induce your opponent to power up, while you ride, contain it or disperse it in some way, he will be burning energy, not double yours, but to a power of yours.

How you do it is, as I have said, through making him carry your weight for you. When he attacks use the force of inertia to slow rather than try to stop him. When he attacks try to think of this, I must engage him with more muscles than he is using against me. If his attack brings into force five of his muscles, defend it with eight or even better ten. You do not have to count them just think something simple such as, if he attacks with one arm then I defend it with an arm and something else such as bringing my chest into contact too.

However, you must not let your opponent know that you are trying to tire him otherwise he may turn the tables on you. Do it in such a way that at the start that he thinks he is winning and gaining on you. Too late he realises his error and you have tricked and tired him.

If you manage to tire an opponent who is very strong, and aware that he is so, make him suffer his tiredness so that he remembers it. If you manage to make him tap when you have exhausted him, cover any tiredness you may have and quickly make him fight again. He will probably try to use all his remaining strength to see if he can destroy you with a powerful burst. You must be ready for this and ride it out as if it were nothing. He is not only trying to beat you, it is about strategy. He thought that he could beat you through sheer strength. You have challenged that belief but not yet destroyed it. You must keep at him over and over while he is tired to destroy his will and confidence in his strength. If you manage to do this he will resist you less next time. He may even not use his strength against you as he no longer believes it is effective.

If in his exhaustion he exclaims at how he cannot believe your strength you must shrug and give him nothing, hiding your own tiredness.

Sometimes you cannot tire an opponent and this will be very dangerous. You will have to doubly rely on technique. You must resist the urge to snatch at an opportunity too soon that he can shrug out of and then catch you in a vulnerable position.

You could try to induce an error. If he presents you with one, you may have to put all your attention to detail and all your strength into carrying your submission off.

A better strategy is to focus your attack. You maybe weaker overall but if your attack is focused narrowly it may give you a result. Often a strong opponent is not used to this and may panic. You may have again to fully commit for it to be a success.

∞✝∞
Pressure.

Create pressure on your opponent to try to induce him to make a mistake. It is not enough that you hold your opponent down. To win you will often have to force a mistake. This can be done direct from a good hold down as it creates it's own pressure, or if that is not sufficient you must create it by making an attack on him.

The simplest is to press your elbow or the blade of your forearm into him. As you press down you ignore your forearm or give it only ten percent of your concentration and concentrate on waiting for him to come out of his defence or to make a mistake.

∞‡∞
Rhythm/Tempo.

Rhythm is little discussed in fighting but is very important. Each fight can be seen to have a rhythm and the person who controls it is the one who dominates. The two fighters end up synchronising to a rhythm. If they did not, the fight would be quickly over.

If you find yourself in a fight where you are being dictated too, chasing to keep up, reacting to all your opponents' moves, regain the dominance of the rhythm of the fight. Just being aware of rhythm and thinking about it will help you.

Often the fight will happen at one pace, but if you want to win you will utilise changes in rhythm to gain advantage over your opponent. For example if the fight is happening to a particular rhythm with move and counter move you can gain an advantage by moving very rapidly to a surprising place.

If you find a fighter difficult to deal with and don't know why, it will be because of differences in rhythm.

∞‡∞
Chasing the arm.

More often than not in submission grappling you are facing your opponent's arm. You can chase this arm no matter where your opponent turns or goes. Not only does this constant pressure tire his arm and make it vulnerable there becomes an inevitability to your attack, to your victory, that wears away at your opponent until he finally gives you the arm that you want.

∞‡∞
Do not give him what he wants.

One good tactic is not to let your opponent do what he wants. For example, if he is in a good position and starts to wrap up your arm, unwrap it immediately. Often he will become trapped in his desire to complete his aim and try over and over to get the same thing. If he tries ten times you must resist ten times. You need to resist the urge to give in and fight equally as hard each time and at the same time look for your own opportunities.

Once an opponent has given up on his attempt at a finish he will be disheartened and maybe vulnerable to your own attack or attempt at reversing him to a more favourable position for you.

Another example is when your opponent is on top of you and decides to move around. Placing your hand on his hip and locking out your arm stops him moving. It is surprising at how quickly the opponent becomes frustrated with this and gives up his move or gives away an opportunity.

∞‡∞
Give him what he wants.

The opposite of this is that it is often beneficial to let your opponent get what he wants and lead him into your trap. This is particularly the case if you can induce a temporary false struggle so that when he is getting what he thinks he wants he starts to relax or he rushes in too quickly. In this state you can realise your plan and take him completely by surprise.

∞‡∞
Arms and legs, shoulders and hips, centres.

Movement centres on the hips. If you are losing it's probably because you are concentrating too much on your opponent's arms and shoulders. Your defence starts by knowing where your opponent's hips are and controlling them.

∞‡∞
Listen to what your opponent says.

Listening to what your opponent says, particularly after a fight is very informative. Most people only pay little attention and miss information that can be like gold to you. Your opponent may say, "If you would have just held that position a little longer, I was about to give up". "When you hold me in that position I can hardly breathe". "When you get me in that position I find it really difficult to deal with and I was glad you changed it". "I hate any pressure on my neck, I always tap quickly".

This kind of information is priceless. Most fighters don't listen and make us of it and miss out on major opportunities.

∞‡∞
Float.

If your opponent is underneath you and is moving wildly, or tries to spin taking you with him, you may find it advantageous to touch the floor instead of him and float above him, choosing your time to drop back down on him. This move surprises your opponent. It is a form of withdrawal.

∞‡∞
Riding.

If you are on top of your opponent and he tries to buck and throw you off you can ride his movements, like a rodeo rider rides a bucking horse.

For each of his big or his micro movements you can choose to resist or fall back and you can choose by how much you resist or are prepared to fall back. Generally at the start when his strength is high you let him throw you around more, letting your weight do the work to tire him as much as you can. Generally you hang on in there like the rodeo rider. You may have to use a strong grip and a lot of strength to do that but it will be a lot less than he is using. As his strength begins to wane you resist his movements more and more until you finally subdue him. Then you can turn the tables on him and turn to attack.

What is crucial when he is throwing you around is your centres. You let him throw you about in such a way that, even though it may not look it, you are in control. You use your centre to make it tiring for him and his centre. He can move your entire body around but your centre remains dominant over him. Even if he has the strength to throw you completely off, i.e. throw your centre away from his, You should be prepared and the instant you land you scramble back on top of him before he can adjust his position. Your centre is now back over his, he is exhausted and you are fresh and he has to start over again.

∞‡∞
Mimic.

If someone is exceptional at a particular technique get them to show you it and talk you through it. Often you will be able to mimic them and your own technique improves. Mimicking is how children learn and they learn a lot and very quickly.

Sometimes you have to admit that you will never be as good at one particular technique as someone else. This may be due to a number of reasons, fitness, flexibility, strength, even just body size. If this is the case, do not worry, be happy with being competent at that technique and look to become exceptional in a few things yourself that become real weapons for you. You may find that something you feel you are merely competent at has real shock value for you as no one expects you to do it and it gets you surprising wins.

∞‡∞
Distance.

Movement is linked to speed and distance. There are advantageous positions and dangerous positions. There are effective distances and ineffective distances and movement brings about the opportunities.

If you are on the bottom your opponent will often try to lift himself up off you to gain the required distance for his attack. You can stop this and the best way is to let gravity help you, even though you are on the bottom.

How you do this is you let your arm go around his neck in the manner of a strong loose rope, not gripping and loosing energy. When he tries to rise you solidify your arm like a bent metal bar. If he wants to rise he has to lift you with him. This would tire him but would also not give him the distance he required for his attack so he gives up.

Alternatively, if he rises you can lift yourself off the ground raising your body to his by arching your back, thereby not giving him the distance between you he required again. Of course you also block his hips and leg movements with your own.

In a similar way he may have top position and need distance from you to create a finish either by falling or rolling away from you. You can counter this in a number of ways. By throwing off his grip of you, by holding onto him and keeping him close or most surprisingly to him, by throwing yourself in the same direction and keeping the distance between you closed.

∞‡∞
Centres.

You may win a fight with an arm bar and feel very little in the fight, or it might not be fought on the edges, it may be fought in your very centres.

In essence it is all physics. It is all about the movement of opposing forces. A key factor in this is your centre and his centre. If you are in a hold down position it is all about the competition between your centres. If you are on top you are crushing him and his centre with yours. He should be trying to protect his centre from you and look for opportunities to weaken and move yours and move his against you.

∞‡∞
Indecision.

When you have practiced for a long time you should be able to detect indecision in your opponent. When you see this for sure you must move quickly and decisively. Your opponent will be paralysed momentarily and your move will be easy and it will be too late for him.

∞‡∞
Put your hand on his face.

Covering your opponents face so that he cannot breathe easily or see can cause your opponent to panic and give away something to you, such as an arm bar. If you develop your other senses you will not be susceptible to this and know that it is just a trick. Even though your eyes are covered you will know the position of your opponent's body and its intended moves.

∞‡∞
Assessment.

If you are fighting someone new you can make an assessment of him by tapping his outstretched hand or alternatively fainting to move towards him. You note his reaction and repeat the process, looking to see if he reacts in the same way. This is his natural reaction and not something he can prepare to trick you with. He will not even be aware that he is reacting in a particular way or that you are setting him up. If he reacts and moves in a particular way each time you can make an instant strategy to take advantage of this movement because as you tap his hand for the third time you know what he will do and you can appear with him in that place.

If he does not react and is confident you will know he is an experienced fighter and you will have to be on your guard for his traps and strategies against you.

∞✝∞
Destroy his base/position.

Because it is a general rule that you need to gain position before submission, you can use this in reverse. If your opponent is trying to get a submission on you, you maybe able to stop it by destroying his base, his position, rather than freeing the area attacked. He may for instance have your arm wrapped up for an arm bar but it you destroy his base he has no leverage to enforce it.

∞✝∞
Align him.

Align him to your advantage. For example, he has you in side position with him in the dominant top position. You adjust the position so that it is more advantageous to you by putting your arm over the back of his neck and squeezing your shoulder and forearm together. He adjusts his head to make it more comfortable for him but puts his body in a better position for you to attack his head and neck and for you to try your reversals and escapes.

You can tell a good fighter because he will naturally not let you do this.

In reverse you do not let him align you. For example, you are in his guard and he moves his hips out to align you for his attacks. You do not defend against the attacks; you bring your hips back together. You do this continually if necessary if you fear his attack. You frustrate and tire him into a mistake. You do not let him frustrate or tire you.

6 TECHNIQUES

1.   The Start.
2.   Construction.
3.   Anchors.
4.   Pins.
5.   Wraps.
6.   Stones.
7.   One hand as two.
8.   Knee on belly.
9.   Holding on 1.
10.   Holding on 2.
11.   Break Grip.
12.   Breathing 1.
13.   Breathing 2.
14.   Levers and pulleys 1.
15.   Levers and pulleys 2.
16.   Inertia.
17.   Straight arms.
18.   The art of deflection.
19.   Distance and feints.
20.   Weight.
21.   Leg attacks.
22.   Pre-moves.
23.   Senses.
24.   Finish it.
25.   Giving up.
26.   Removing blocks.
27.   Perfect and cumbersome.
28.   Bridging.
29.   Rolling out.
30.   Create pressure.
31.   Friction.

TECHNIQUES.
∞╪∞

The Start.

The start is a constant. You will do this more than anything else. I have always been surprised that people do not study it more. A good start is one of the most important things in your fight. If you can win the start and gain an advantage it will greatly help your chances of winning. I repeat, greatly increase your chance of winning. What classes as a good start is to topple your opponent over and take a dominant position.

Grip. You can gain an advantage in trying to topple your opponent over by having a better grip than him. You will find opponents who differ greatly in this from the one extreme where he does not mind any grip you take of him, to the other where he will absolutely fight you full out to stop you getting any kind of grip of you and try to make no engagement with you until they have a grip as hard as iron and others who fall somewhere in between.

Those who fight hardest for the best grip often come from a judo background. This is an over commitment due to how fights finish in judo. In judo you gain points from flipping your opponent or holding him down. In grappling this is not the end; submission is the only end. Flipping your opponent or holding him down may turn out to be of no value. In grappling or other fighting you should not commit so much to this kind of grip as it does not allow you to disengage as easy or launch or defend strikes.

In trying to topple him over there is only pushing or pulling, the direction of your push or pull and then, least understood, how high or low you are. Even though there are only three things those three can be put together in an infinite number of variations and combinations.

You may go on the following journey of development.

At the start you simply try to push or pull your opponent over to the left or right in a competition of strength. You then realise that you can push or pull not just left or right, but to any point of the compass, all three hundred and sixty degrees.

When you feel him resisting your push or pull you learn to reverse your attack in the opposite direction. You can reverse this backwards and forwards. One particular variation of this is the following. You are trying to pull your opponent over. You get him leaning far over but cannot get him to topple so you give up pulling. His body falls back towards a central position and as it does so you surprisingly push him hard helping him on his way. You use his own momentum. He goes past the equilibrium point he thought he was going to stop at, hastens over the opposite side and you topple him. It is natural to feel great joy when this happens.

Another stepping stone of development is the use of sacrifice. You will be taught this and have to practice it. What you do is let him push or pull you and as you fall you reverse him and take a dominant position. It is best to take him by surprise. One good way is if he is pushing you then you strongly resist it so that he pushes very hard and you suddenly give way. He collapses towards you and you use his own momentum to reverse him. This is helpful with strong or heavier opponents. If he is committed to his push he will be lost in mid-air and unable to resist you.

One method is to suddenly stop him. He will be confused and before he can orientate himself you get him in motion in the direction you want.

Curves. An advanced version of taking someone to the floor is not to push or pull in straight lines but in curves. The initial push or pull will be in straight lines but as your opponent moves you change to an ever tightening arc. If you are pulling him towards you and the arc narrows, once he begins to topple you can now push or pull him nearer or further away from you to get him into your favoured position on the floor.
The reason for the arc is because it is very difficult to resist. If the point of your attack was in one direction he could pull back in the opposite direction for maximum effect for him. Because the point of your attack is on curves it continually changes which makes it far more difficult for him to pin point and apply an opposing force..

To understand this, imagine pulling a car on a rope. For maximum effect you would want to be in line with it. Now imagine pulling on the rope at forty five degrees to the car. It would be far more difficult and wasteful of your energy to do this.

You can also use this in your defence if he tries to move you, changing your position slightly to weaken the angle of his attack.

In defence you can resist him with your strength but be ready to react to any changes in direction or strength of his attack. Alternatively you can let him move you. You may lean and let your weight take his force. You can slide over the floor or hop back. He has moved you but to no advantage as you basically have the same position, he has not tipped you over. This dissipates his strength and he has no gain.

A main form of defence is to flatten your base, widen your base. As he attacks you lower yourself and widen the amount of your body in touch with the floor; imagine your body as a pyramid, narrow at the top, wide at the bottom. In effect you have lowered your centre. He will find this very difficult to get you over in this position. The negatives of this position is that if you are much lower than him he can just take top position and dominate you. You are also a long way from turning him over. You sink into this position under his attack staying just low enough to resist it.

It should be remembered that your arms fight each other and your legs push off to give you power, but it is really a fight between dominance of your centres. It can be felt as a fight between two infinitely small points. You are trying to dominate his centre with yours.

∞‡∞
Construction.

A successful lock has a construction to it. Look carefully at this construction. Sometimes your lock has to follow in a particular order and sometimes not. If it does not it is often advantageous to have the second part of your move in place before the first. Your opponent may not be aware that you have half set up the finish move because he is waiting the first part, unaware that it now maybe the last part.

The move can be completed far more quickly and securely with half of it already in place and even though as you move he becomes aware of the danger his response is now too slow and he is left wondering how you managed to trap him.

An example of this is the figure four arm bar. The standard method is to grab his wrist with one hand, then move your other hand under his arm and grab your wrist. You bring the arm to the best position and then twist the arm. It is such an obvious potent threat that everyone hides their arms from it. It is often advantageous to work the second arm into place first under your opponents arm. In itself there is no danger to your opponent in this and he will not particularly resist your movement, but this second arm is now in place. If his arm comes out for whatever reason you can spring your other arm across, catch the wrist of your arm that is already in place and take the arm bar before he is aware.

31

∞‡∞
Anchors.

To secure a position you may drop an anchor. If you are on top of your opponent he will try and move position to escape. His hips are most important in this. If, for example, you put your hand on the floor by the side of his hip and he tries to move his hip away from you it will be blocked by your hand. You do not have to grip him and waste energy; you can let friction and your weight distribution do the job for you. It is truly like dropping an anchor over the side of a ship.

∞‡∞
Pins.

A pin is similar to an anchor. It does a similar job only this time you pin down a part of your opponent so that either he cannot move that part of himself in relation to the floor, or to the rest of his body, depending on what you want to do. In many ways it is better than an anchor. An anchor merely blocks the movement of your opponent; where as a pin does that, but also hurts him, sometimes to the point where he taps or gives you an easy follow up submission.

You may do this for a number of reasons; for example, to stop him doing what he wants to do. You maybe in the middle of a fluid fight and he is trying to come around your back into a dangerous position for you. You halt his attack by pinning his head. As he tries to continue his progress he starts to stretch his own neck and realises he has to give up his attack and fall back. Holding his chin in your hand is good for this.

You may pin part of his body so that your finish will be stronger and work. For example, if you are doing the simple arm lock you have to pin his body flat to the floor with your own chest otherwise he simply turns towards his vulnerable arm and rescues it. Another good idea is to kneel on his limbs. This pins him so that he cannot move, takes away the use of a limb and, of course, hurts.

∞‡∞
Wraps.

A wrap is where you use your arms or legs to go around your opponent trapping his arms and legs to him. You may do it to stop him attacking you with his trapped arms and legs. In wrapping him it also narrows his base and puts pressure on him. Because you have wrapped him and narrowed him you may be able to reverse him. You may also be able to work a submission.

A strong version of this is where you slide your hand under him and use his weight as well. When you do this you must have your body and weight distributed in a way he cannot roll you. This can be very frustrating for your opponent. They are wasting energy and not getting anywhere.

∞✝∞
Stones.

When you are on top of your opponent you can make life difficult for him by placing your fist underneath him. You lay your weight on him to force him onto your fist. We all know the feeling of having a stone in our shoe; it feels painful and we imagine the stone is enormous even though when we take our shoe off it turns out to be tiny. If you do this successfully he will not be able to escape your fists and will have to suffer them. Some people react severely to this and have a strong dislike of it. They will arch their back in agony to try to avoid them and destroy the defensive position they had. You may change the position of your fists to chase the most destructive position for him. He may submit at this point or you maybe able to move to a submission he has offered while he has arched his back and his defence is destroyed.

You must be careful in using your fist as a stone as it can trap your hand underneath him. You need to make sure you that he cannot turn you or that you can withdraw your hand if necessary.

∞✝∞
One hand as two.

You can often use one hand as two. If you put one arm around someone's back and squeezed with it they would feel hardly anything. If you put both your arms around them, locked your hands together and then squeezed it would be very strong. If you can grip something your one hand is like two hands in grappling.

If your hand is on your own chest he could grab it and move it with his two hands, but if you grab your clothes your hand becomes like two hands gripping together and he cannot move it. This is a very useful principle and has many applications.

For instance he may wrap up your one arm with his two in an arm bar. This one arm cannot defend against two by itself, however if you simply grab hold of your clothing with your hand it gains the strength of two hands.

∞✝∞

Knee on belly.

A good example of the combination of many of the above is in the knee on belly position. Many people teach that you put your shin across your opponent's stomach with your foot touching his side so that there is no gap. This is so that your opponent may not put his hand in that gap and spin the position. A better position than this is to put the ball of your knee in the middle and pit of his stomach. At the same time you put your hand under his head and your other hand grips his clothing at his hip. You then pull with both arms and drive your knee into him. If you lift his head up so that his chin sticks into his chest it also takes away forty percent of his strength. He can no longer spin out of the position and he has to suffer your knee.

If he has the character and strength to try to push your knee off his stomach you let him and simply switch your attack to your other knee and place this on his upper chest or even his neck or jaw. He now has to push this off, aware that as he does you are only going to put your other knee into him. When he pushes you off it only helps you spin to the other. After doing this a number of times you will find it advantageous to switch to the following position. You place one knee on his stomach and one on his chest at the same time and grab his clothing at his hip and his shoulder and straighten your back to close to vertical to drive your knees in. This is a more stable position and allows far quicker access to a finish on his arms. You alternatively switch your weight and the attack to each knee as he tries to relieve the pressure off each. He will tire and give you opportunities to finish him by taking his arms.

∞✝∞

Holding 1.

Truly it is difficult for your opponent to stop gripping and holding when it is to his advantage to do so. If your opponent is holding you, you may spin your position to your advantage and he will not let go of holding you to adjust his position until it is too late.

Also, you may use the fact that your opponent is holding onto you in the following way. You may be on top of him with his arms around your back pulling you towards him. If you put your elbow on his jaw and crush down he will still continue to pull you towards him unaware for a long time that he is helping to crush his own jaw. By the time he realises what he is doing he is tired, disheartened and you are ready to move quickly and take advantage.

Letting go is of the mind, not of the hand.

∞✝∞
Holding on 2.

You should be pleased when your opponent grabs hold of you. You should not flinch or try to pull away. Your body is now freely joined with his, yes, but at his expense. It is the nature of inexperienced people to think that because they have hold of you they are winning. He does not realise his arms are holding you but your arms are free. Through his touch you can feel his strength, experience and know his body position and the potential movement of his limbs. With patience you move your body position to an advantageous one and you win.

∞✝∞
Break Grip.

If your opponent grips hold of your arm or wrist you may wish to remove your arm from his grip. This will not always be the case as by gripping hold of you he may have lost the use of his hand for no gain. Many inexperienced people move their arms about vigorously trying to free themselves and achieve nothing. If you want to free your arm you pull it towards the finger and thumb opening of his hand and preferably pull your arms towards your own body, for strength. It is the weak point of his grip. In this way it is surprising how easy it is to free the arm.

∞✝∞
Breathing 1.

Breathing is very important in submission grappling. It is best when you can ignore it and it controls itself. There are three forces against your breathing. The first is your mental state. If you panic and do not think wisely your breathing will become inefficient. The second is your physical state drawing on your breathing for oxygen and energy. At times you may have to lessen your physical exertions to enable your breathing to supply these requirements adequately. You must do this in such a way that your opponent does not gain an advantage either physically or mentally by being aware that you are struggling. The third is that your opponent may put strain and pressure on your body in such a way as to limit your breathing capacity. As said before you can make minor adjustments to your position that will increase your breathing capacity.

One important thing to be aware of is that if you are struggling for breath you need to do what is counter intuitive. You will be tempted to try to get more oxygen by repeatedly breathing shallow and quickly. What you need to do is breathe everything out and you will naturally breathe in. The first breath will be very difficult but you must do it and continue the process until you are flush with oxygen. What you are doing is getting rid of bad air that is full of carbon dioxide and has little oxygen. You are making your lungs far more efficient and healthy.

As in all things though, it is far better to dominate and win the fight and never get caught in a bad position.

∞✝∞

Breathing 2.

Listen and feel what is happening to your opponent's body, particularly to their breathing. This may tell you how your hold down is doing and when it is particularly damaging to them. Try to take their breath from them.

Often an opponent will give you a signal that he is about to make a big move, for example, try to throw you off, by taking a breath and holding it. He may also even have a few practice runs at it while he tries to give himself the confidence to go for it for real. Needless to say, if you know a move is coming you can prepare for it and set a trap for him.

One different and interesting thing that you can do is the following. If you sense him building up to a big move, just before he is about to do it you can innocently move your position a little. This will cause him to stop, wondering what you are doing. His adrenalin was peaking and now it will dissipate. He will be confused and have to start over. This tires, frustrates and disheartens him. You will be surprised how many times you can do this.

Counter to this is the fact that you should give nothing away by your own movements and breathing, unless you are setting a trap.

∞✝∞
Levers and pulleys 1.

The genius Archimedes showed us the way with the importance of levers. You need to develop an affinity for seeing and feeling how they work, how to use them to create pressure on your opponent and how to relieve pressure on yourself. For example, if you put your forearm across the jaw line of your opponent and press down it will give him pain. However, if you cup your hand under the ball of his shoulder and use that as a fulcrum you can create even more pressure. Levers are extremely important and need to be understood.

One of the most important points for your levers is the ground. For a long time sail ships could not sail into the window until a genius invented a particular sail that enabled the ship to do so. It may sound impossible but there is a way you can use the ground while you are crushing your opponent into the ground.

A good idea when you are practicing a finish move is to think through your body to where the fulcrum is. You will naturally focus on the point of finish looking for ways to improve it. The fulcrum point is usually adjusted unconsciously and is not often placed in the forefront of the conscious mind. It would be a good idea to try this.

∞✝∞
Levers and pulleys 2.

An arm closer to your body has greater strength than at a distance from it. If your opponent attacks your arm, pull it closer to your body. Turning towards the arm pulls it in its wake further away from him and gains protection under your body. When you have turned, bending at the hip and curving at the spine creates a hole taking the arm further away from him along with everything else this does.

As I have said, if you can grab hold of your clothing your hand has the strength of two arms. If you cannot do any of this you may have to rescue your arm with your other arm.

∞✝∞
Inertia.

Often it is not necessary to remove your limb from an attack. Often it is sufficient to hold its position. This is particularly the case with wrist or finger locks. If someone tries a wrist lock, do not try to remove your attacked hand, bring your other hand to its rescue. All you do is hold your attacked hand with your other hand to keep its position. Remember, your opponent has to bend your hand to make you tap. It is far easier for you to hold its position than it is for him to force it to move. This is using the force of inertia. You hold it in position until he gives up. If your hand has been twisted a little you may have to shake it to get the blood flowing before you can use it again.

∞‡∞
Straight arms.

If your opponent is trying to come towards you and you do not wish him too a locked straight arm will stop him. Due to the distance required to lock your arm out this will not be available to you often, but can be used excellently on occasion.

You need to be careful of giving your opponent the opportunity of getting an arm bar but used correctly your opponent will not be able to approach you or knock your arm away.

∞‡∞
The art of deflection.

A new fighter meets every attack head on and is soon exhausted and led into traps. An experienced fighter will sometimes take an attack head on but more often uses the art of deflection.

An excellent fighter knows exactly by how much to deflect an attack to render it useless.

Deflecting rather than stopping an attack conserves your energy and tires your opponent. For your opponent it is like taking a wrong turn on a car journey. You have to back up and re-find your route. It is tiring and frustrating.

You can use deflection to draw your opponent's attack into a trap. Often he will not know his attack is being deflected, he actually thinks it is working until it is too late, he can not withdraw.

∞╪∞
Distance and Feints.

Use of distance is very important. There are three types of distance. You can be at a particular distance and you are not engaged and your opponent will feel safe. As you close the distance to him he becomes less safe. There is a narrow area where you may or may not engage by stepping forward. There is the final area where if you step into it your opponent has to engage you. You can make use of these three areas to try to gain an advantage or control of the fight.

You can enter the area where your opponent has to engage you at a moment that is advantageous to you. Many of your full moves are preceded by a faint move beforehand. His process will be to hit full readiness physically and mentally and then when you don't go through with it, his readiness plummets as he relaxes. You try to induce your opponent to experience that process so that you can get him when he is relaxing. For example you might faint to close the distance. Your opponent starts towards your probe and you withdraw into the half zone. As your opponent starts to drop back and relax you spring through the distance at a speed far quicker than your probe attack and catch him by surprise. While he flinches and does not take a proper position you are prepared and act correctly.

There is also a second way you can gain advantage over him to do with position. You psychologically confuse him over your position. He suddenly finds too late that you are in the zone where he should engage you but thought you were still in the safe zone.

Faints. You do it by fainting to enter the engagement zone in a rhythmical way. He becomes entrapped in his responses to your rhythm. You feint to drop back your probe forward as you have done previously but don't you actually step forward. He has a moments surprise as he finds you in the wrong place and may even admire your move as you take the advantage of him.

Some opponents will not fall for it easily but others will time and time again even increasingly so. This may sound unbelievable but it is truly possible. You should use it over and over again until he finds a way of mastering it. Usually he will do this by getting you to fail yourself rather than him finding his own cure.

∞┼∞
Weight.

You need to learn the correct use of your weight. Even though you are smaller, lighter and less strong than your opponent you move him and he does not move you. Even though you are lighter than your opponent he complains about how heavy you are but when he is on top of you there is no weight. This is the correct use of your weight.

Weight is not a fixed thing even for the same weight. You may lift a heavy metal bar quite easily, but a large balloon filled with liquid of the same weight would be more difficult to lift. You may have no difficulty lifting a chair that is close to you, but at arm's length you may injure yourself trying to lift it. You may push off a heavy load easily, but removing a piece of paper can be very hard if it is sticky. You can lift a solid easily but how much water can you lift with no container? So when you want to lift him he is a stiff metal bar and when he wants to lift you, then you are a liquid for him.

∞┼∞
Leg attacks.

On the subject of leg locks, if you can master them your opponents will fear you and will always have them in mind, to your advantage. Again, if you are having great difficulty with an opponent, usually someone stronger than you, you may be able to turn the tables on them by developing your leg locks.

∞┼∞
Pre-moves.

This is a complex idea and can start as a physical or a mental thing.

Mental. Most things in this section start off in the sub-conscious. You feel your opponent is about to do something and this gives you the time and opportunity to react. With repetition you become more consciously aware of it and can look for his pre-moves, his tells, that give you the signal that he is about to act. These come from his sub-conscious. You may wish to stop your opponent's hand reaching out to you. You may stop his hand with your hand, but you can stop it even getting close to you by blocking his upper arm, or even his shoulder from moving.

Physical. A particular move may have a pre-move. The most obvious of these is a push or a punch that involves pulling the arm back before it fires forwards. If you can spot and block the pre-move you stop the actual move. You can even look for these chains of events by back tracking over previous experiences rather than just waiting to come across them.

You may be able to induce a response from your opponent by doing particular things, either physical or mental.

∞‡∞
Senses.

You may wonder where to put your eyes when you fight. This is a good question when grappling. You should not put them in any particular place. In fact you should try to take your mind away from your sight a little as a sense. We are dominated by our sense of sight to the detriment of the other senses. You should try to encourage the use of your other senses, particularly touch and sound. The predominance of sight will vary during a fight depending on your use of it. You should be able to tune in and out of your different senses as required in the fight. At times, when you do not have use of it at all and require more from touch and sound, you may even close your eyes. You may find that your sense of smell disappears. It is your subconscious switching it off as unimportant for the moment. When you come out of an intense fight you might feel surprise as you suddenly regain a sense of smell, and other senses you had switched off as unimportant.

In this manner it is a good training method to fight with your eyes closed; it encourages the use of your other senses. In this way you can learn to know your opponents move when he thinks of it and not when he executes it.

If you find you are fighting with one hundred percent of your focus on sight it could be that your opponent is intimidating you, dominating you. You will need to analyse this. It may be that you are making the correct and only possible decision; it may be that you have to fight your own mind to overcome it and get it to work more efficiently and better for you.

∞‡∞
Finish it.

If you have your opponent suffering you must press home your attack and not let him recover. If you are the type of timid fighter who finds this difficult, think that you are doing him a favour by ultimately lessening his suffering by finishing the fight quickly.

In Roman Gladiator contests a winner was supposed to wait for the royal signal, thumbs up for life, thumbs down for death. Many gladiators had to let their opponent live only to lose to them in future, face the same fate and end up dying. Many gladiators learned to deliver a fatal, maiming or crippling blow before that so it could not happen to them as they were suspicious of it.

If you let a submission go and then lose to your opponent, do you think he will believe you had him and let him go?

∞‡∞

Giving up.

At times you have your opponent trapped in a hold that you just can't quite finish; it maybe that your opponent is able to resist the finish because of his position, or strength, or a combination of both. Maybe you are considering giving up the position because you are tiring or suffering under his returned pressure. This can be great, for example you may have his arm wrapped but you are underneath him and he is crushing down on you.

You need to seriously consider not giving up on the position before you give it away. You may not get such an advantageous position again. It maybe with one final effort or adjustment to the position, such as a spin, you can make it work. One more try when your opponent thinks you have given up may just work. If you pull it off when you considered giving up it will be something that will stay with you and you will not give up so easily in the future.

Having said that, if it is obvious your attack is not going to work you will need to save energy and prepare for your opponent's move as you release him. Try to gain the advantage. Maybe you can use your attack as purely a hold while you figure out your best move. Also do not let your opponent sense any disheartenment over your lack of success, again, unless you are pretending for a trap.

∞‡∞

Removing blocks.

If your opponent tries to restrict your movement by putting his hand on you, for example, your hip, you may remove this in the following ways;

By knocking it away with your close arm.

You may twist around to rock the surface he has his hand on in such a way his hand slips enough for you to move.

You may remove it by the surprising use of your far arm, but be careful with this and do not let him catch you crossing yourself.

You may induce him to remove it by attacking him in such a way that he has to withdraw the arm to defend against the attack.

You may change your move, for example, going in the opposite direction away from his hand, even using the position of his hand as an advantage.

∞✝∞

Perfect and cumbersome.

Many fighters who become quite good like to try for perfection in their techniques. They look good as they fight and enjoy looking good, but this can hide a weakness and another way of fighting. For want of a better term we can call it cumbersome.

The problem in looking for perfection is that those who do will pass up opportunities at finishing their opponent because they literally do not see them. They may look at their opponent's body position and think it is not in the correct position yet rather than it is close enough and I can now make it work.

A beautiful finish is lovely to see, lovely flowing movements, beautiful arcs and angles. They are the ones that if you were making a training film, you would choose them. A cumbersome finish is different and can be found where a pretty one can not. Some good fighters train themselves out of this type of finish.

A cumbersome finish involves perhaps grabbing your opponents arm out of position and forcing it and fighting it into the correct position for a finish. It looks cumbersome because your movement is not one beautiful arc; your movement wobbles from side to side. This is very important. You would not have the strength to pull it direct to a finish, but you do have the strength to move it to the side and a little also in the direction you want. The first movement will be the biggest and wildest. As you bring it back and forth closer to the required position the movements become less wild, smaller and your position becomes stronger for you.

You may have a little disappointment that your finish was cumbersome and not pretty. Your opponent may try to feed you the feeling that it wasn't a good finish, it was ugly and even that it was unworthy. You need to firmly ignore this and appreciate your technique as a valid technique that he is, in his ignorance, not seeing. It feels awkward and cumbersome, but it is not; in its way it will be a perfectly executed thing of beauty. Let him have his misguided pride while you take the victory. It is worth remembering that in a hard fight and a real fight your finishes are far more likely to be cumbersome than pretty. Your opponent will not let you do a beautiful finish. Beautiful finishes are usually inflicted on an opponent you are beating easily so which finish is truly more worthless a beautiful one or one that is cumbersome?

∞✝∞

Bridging.

A bridge is where you arch your back up off the floor onto your shoulder, shoulders or head, like a bridge. If your opponent tries for a position or submission you may be able to frustrate him by bridging him up. You may even throw him off. This is a very strong position for you. Your bridge will weaken his base, maybe destroying his move in itself. Also you can bridge more one side of your body than the other. This has the effect of, for example, hiding the arm he wants to attack away from him under your body. You can collapse your bridge back down when you feel it is appropriate and bridge again if he tries the same thing again.

∞✝∞

Rolling out.

Rather than resisting your opponent's move, or trying to undo it, you can roll out. This is a general tactic. What you do is go in the same direction your opponent wants you to go, but faster than him and that gives you your escape. This can be desperate and dangerous for you. If anything gets tangled as you move you could injury yourself. If your opponent knows your movement he may be waiting for you when you come out of the movement. It can be very surprising to your opponent to go with him.

∞‡∞
Create Pressure.

Whatever position you are in you should be looking for a way to create pressure on your opponent. Every possible moment should be difficult for him. Every step hard.

∞‡∞
Friction.

In submission grappling friction is very important. In all your moves you are touching something. Friction works in the following ways;

If you have a block on the floor you need to give it a certain force before it will move. Before that force it will not move.

If a block is already moving you will have to give it a certain force to stop it.

Your touch with friction will be so automatic that it is difficult to analyse its use. You will use friction where it does not break to push off or to stop your movement. At times you may use sliding friction to slow and control you and your opponent's movements and this is more subtle.

7 PSYCHOLOGY

1. Psyching your opponent out – Physically led.
2. Psyching your opponent out – Psychologically led.
3. When someone tries to psych out you.
4. Flow.
5. Desperateness.
6. Ultimate desperateness.
7. The same thing.
8. Fixed and flexible thinking.
9. Emptiness.
10. Zoning out.
11. Getting into character.
12. Superstitions and routines.
13. Desire.
14. Small thoughts – Big ideas.
15. Mental strength.
16. Courage?
17. Psychopaths.
18. Fear.
19. Relentlessness.
20. Exhaustion.
21. Pain.

PSYCHOLOGY.

Psyching your opponent out - Physically led.

Winning before you start. Some opponents are more easily psychologically destroyed than others. Often, if you are good, your opponent is defeated before you lay a hand on him. He may know it and it will be obvious to him and visible to everyone, or alternatively he may not be conscious of it but fights you as if constrained in a glass box, unaware of opportunities all around him and blind to your weaknesses. You have psyched him out without doing anything, just by being invincible before him in his mind.

At other times you may be fighting an opponent who appears phenomenal, who is in the process of a devastating and flawless attack. They appear unbeatable and you are helpless against them if they follow their strategy through. When there is no physical solution to you there may be a psychological solution. After all, there is always a solution. When you have tried everything you can think of to directly stop him physically and it has not worked you can try something indirectly. You need to get him to change, to break his own strategy. It is not him that is invincible; it is his strategy, his system and you need to break the loop of his thinking. It maybe invincible from the outside, but it is not from the inside.

You can disrupt his psychology in a physically led way, doing something, anything, physically to distract him from his present task.

You could repeatedly do something such as just pushing on his head or pulling on his arm to goad, annoy and so distract him. This can break his concentration and once he is distracted you must turn the tables in some way quickly before he remembers to go back to his assault.

You could do something quickly that makes him flinch. While his mind is stunned you take advantage and move.

One particular physical way is of the following type; just as he is about to move, right at the start of it, the point of change, you do something random that is unconnected to what he is doing such as simply tap him on his arm firmly. This will often completely stop him in his tracks while he tries to process the significance of your move. This can be even better than a usual expected defence. He would be expecting that. Something random makes his mind search. He will be thinking, 'Why did he do that? He must have a reason?' If he launches the attack again do the same thing you did again. You should find that if it stops him once it stops him again. He will be thinking, 'He has done it again. What can he see that I can't see?'

With luck he could doubt so much that he gives up or is not as convincing an attack. However he may shake off his doubt and go back the attack fully determined to avoid your distractions. You must judge this and act while he is distracted either taking his body or his mind further and further away from what he had.

∞‡∞

Psyching your opponent out – Mentally led.

It maybe that your opponent has launched an attack on you and you are struggling to resist it physically and know that he could be about to beat you. While you cannot stop his move physically you may be able to destroy it by pure psychology.

A surprising way I have found to be very effective is to flatter the very move that is destroying you. Ask him how he does it or why is he so good at it. Any form of question that gets him to think of his move and analyse it. Suddenly he cannot do it successfully anymore. Any move is so complex, built up of so many micro-parts that are 'felt' in the subconscious rather than known in the conscious that to describe it will be impossible. When he thinks of it his mind tries to break it down into parts and it becomes like a motorcycle he has taken apart, it is almost impossible for him to put back together successfully. That is what you have done to him, you have moved it from his subconscious mind to his conscious and they are two very different 'people'. You should find that asking him this one question means that he, at least temporarily, loses the ability to complete the move anywhere near as successfully as before. This should be long enough for your purposes. You may even find that from then on it is not as successful a move for him anymore.

You may doubt the truth of this but it can easily be proved to you, for example, you may be able to ride a bike, to swim and to walk, so; 'Describe to me the process of how you walk.'

Normally it is a good idea to hide what you are trying to do but conversely another way to destroy his move or his defence is to tell him exactly what you are trying to do. Him thinking about thinking about his strategy is more difficult than him just thinking about his strategy. Again it is about moving it to his conscious mind and out of his subconscious. While he thinks about protecting his strategy or forcing it through, this will also alter his approach to his technique and give you new options and opportunities. The subtle difference, that he will be unaware of, is that whereas before he was inside his system, he is now outside of his system trying to make it work. This will lose him his feel of his move and slow his timing.

Another psychological tactic is to enamour him. These come from a deep well of experience. Many little pieces suddenly and mysteriously slot together. You will doubt the possibility of such a thing, even after you have made the unreal real. For example, I was thinking of attacking my opponents arm. He could see I looked at his arm. I realised there was no way I could get it and I sensed him relax. For no apparent reason I started to stare intently at his arm. He became more and more uneasy and I stared more and more intently at his arm. I had the sensation of him being transfixed before me and I took his arm from an impossible position.

You can get an opponent into a mind-set where he is principally concerned about your attacks then you may induce him to defeat in the following way, you get him to freely give you what you want. This may seem truly unbelievable but you can sense when he will be ready for it.

An example of this is that you have top position and are holding him down. You may wish to take an arm bar on the arm in front of you but due to its position he can defend it or you cannot get it. How you get it is that you get him to simply give it to you himself.

How you induce this trap is in the following way; you go for his arm, even though you know you won't get it and he successfully defends. You give up the attack and let him relax for a second, then you do the same unsuccessful attack again and again he defends. You may do this a number of times until you sense he is ready. This is the important step. After going hard for the arm and not getting it you act as if you have honestly given up the attack and not in any obvious exaggerated way but naturally. What happens next is unbelievable. He relaxes and his arm comes out all by itself into the very vulnerable position you have been trying to force it to, you are ready and waiting and instantaneously you take the arm. It is finished. He will be in total shock and say something like, "I can't believe I did that? Why did I put my arm there"?

Maybe you hypnotised him? Who exactly knows what this is?

∞‡∞
When some one tries to psych out you.

Psychological strength is a quantity like physical strength. Some people have more of it than others but you can train yourself to be stronger. Every hypnotist will tell you some people are easier than others to hypnotise. It can be referred to as character.

If you can smile at his attempt to psych you out and show you are unaffected you will become a mirror for him and he will see his actions as a weakness. If he continues stronger you can make him appear desperate and weaken his character and resolve. He may even lose his temper. Again, do not let this affect you and he will ensure his own downfall.

If someone has this over you then you must burn away what is essentially a fog.

∞‡∞
Flow.

You can only gain flow when you gain experience. It is not an alternate reality it has a feeling of clarity, of hyper reality. If you have ever driven a car with the handbrake on for a time, flow feels like when you take the handbrake off. Flow is a wonderful feeling. Everything is easy and smooth and losing is impossible. You are in the zone. You are not thinking in the normal way, it is more like watching yourself work and talking to yourself. You have time even to admire what you are doing as you go. When you are in a state of flow you let it ride. Who knows how long it will stay, when if ever it will come back. You will have times when you can slip into flow as naturally as putting on a pair of shoes. Just as quickly you can be like a new born lamb disconnected from your own self.

∞‡∞
Desperateness.

Some days you have the opposite of flow when everything feels difficult and nothing goes to plan. Maybe something has put you off your game. You feel disconnected from your own self. When this happens you must fight through it. Always fight. You will have a hanging on feeling. You must hang on. It will gradually get better the longer you persevere.

Afterwards you must remember the feeling of how difficult it was at the start, but how it began to turn for the better. You will be able to draw on this in future. You must not give up without fully fighting. You will gain more satisfaction from winning this fight than you will from a hundred that were easy.

It is similar to pain. It is surprising how much you can actually take, you need to educate yourself. If you survive this fight it will become your new level and you will be proud of yourself. You must have had times where you have been surprised at how quickly and easily someone has tapped and you have felt shame on their behalf. Remember this feeling and use it to push you on to never let it happen to you. You should also remember fights where you could not believe how much punishment someone has taken and not given in and how dangerous you felt this fighter to be. Use this also to spare you on.

In fighting you are aiming to be in complete control, relaxed, in what is known as flow, the zone, linked to the idea of Zen in Japanese. When that happens fighting is easy. Thinking becomes different. The fight happens in slow motion and you know what is going to happen before it happens. Your senses do not happen in the same way. You do not have individual senses like smell or touch or sound, you have one whole sense. You can not tire and you can not feel pain.

The twin to this way of fighting is its opposite, desperateness. This is when everything is against you, you face crushing defeat and exhaustion. All your senses are separate. You feel everything, sight, sound, heat and cold and you feel everything in pain. Your mind will have a visitor who offers you the comfort of defeat and shows you the agony of resisting. It tells you that the only thing stopping you having this wonderful comfort is your own silly pride, and isn't pride wrong?

This is where your training can come to your rescue. If you train yourself well to respond to this situation your body will respond by itself while you are debating and come to your aid and act correctly.

∞‡∞

Ultimate Desperateness.

Imagine for a brief moment that you come home to find men in your house who have raped and killed your wife and children. You should be aware of the power and speed of motion that would be released and the complete black emptiness of what would happen next. How would you come out of the other side of that? The way to see it is as a red button that you can press. Once pressed, whatever would be would be and you would come out of it on the other side, or not. This feeling has a drawing hypnotic power which must be resisted until such a day.

∞‡∞
The Same Thing.

Quite often, if you beat the same opponent with the same technique he will complain to you that that is what you are doing. You may see some fighters become discouraged and put off by this, letting it affect them the next time they fight and not using the technique that gained them victory and suffering defeat instead. This is a ridiculous thing to let happen to you. Beat the same opponent one hundred times in the same way if you wish. It is up to him to learn not for you to change.

∞‡∞
Fixed and Flexible Thinking.

Fixing your mind is a complex thing. Yes a good fighter does not do this. Yes a good fighter has a clear mind and many, many options. A less good fighter does not have as many options and maybe he cannot help fixating on things. Perhaps it is inevitable. Only very few fights are closely fought and ebb and flow. Nearly every fight, the outcome is known before hand.

When you fight in a state of flow it is obviously a two way process, you are able to do it and your opponent is unable to stop you. At times you will not be able to get into flow and you will fixate on a particular technique or position, but is that because you are unable to call on flow or because your opponent does not let you?

If you are up against an excellent, strong fighter, are you not able to call on flow because your opponent does not let you, and this is a bad thing? Or, is it a good thing and your mind is limiting your thought range to help you? Do you have to narrow your focus to give yourself a chance to win?

What happens first? Should you fight the urge to narrow your focus? If you fight in flow you will be winning, but can you get flow no matter who your opponent is? What if your opponent is in flow, do you have to destroy his flow first before you beat him?

These are complex questions and you should think on them deeply.

∞✝∞
Emptiness.

Sometimes I feel I know nothing, I have nothing to teach and feel that if I fought I would not know what to do. I have learned not to be concerned about this. When I feel empty in this way something always comes to me as I turn to teach, something new and good. When I turn to fight I don't try to change my feeling or panic and I win easily. It is like it is not me fighting and feels like I am cheating in some way as my victory comes easily without thought. My finishes can be new versions of old moves or even completely new moves that come easily and quickly as if I am a different fighter altogether. I see complicated moves in three dimensions that I have never seen before.

I have yet to be able to master this feeling and be able to call on it at will. Perhaps it is not possible or advantageous to be able to do so? It is though, like discovering a new horizon, a virgin territory to be explored and gives me a humble feeling. It feels like I have discovered the edge of a new enormous territory. How much more is there to see over the horizon I wonder?

∞✝∞
Zoning out.

There have been times when I have been fighting when I have tried to fight in the zone, zen like, and it has not worked in the following strange way; I have tried to zone out and ended up feeling distant in the fight, absent almost. My opponent has sensed this and moved, taking the initiative. His movements have felt surprising and my reactions slow. It has then been a struggle to get back up to speed and back in the fight. I have had to abandon trying for the zone, which has been difficult, like shaking off sleep and it has left me scrambling.

I have thought about this and had discussions with other people who have had the same feeling. I think where our error lay is indicated by the term zoning out. We had done it incorrectly and placed ourselves out of the present, out of our senses, we had absented ourselves from the fight.

What should happen is that all extraneous thoughts are zoned out and you are left totally in the present, in the here and now, in the fight. Your senses are not switched off, they are left totally clear of distraction.

It is so difficult to induce because when it comes it comes without effort, without trying. It is letting go without letting go. This can only make sense to you if you have felt this.

∞‡∞
Getting into Character.

Some martial artists become martial artists twenty four hours a day. They are out they are on high alert forever looking for danger. I have heard some people say they wish they were attacked or their loved ones attacked so that they could use this. Who wants to live life like that? It would be all consuming, exhausting and not appropriate for modern life. This is not feudal Japan. Personally I like to get into character as I go to martial arts. Obviously I carry that person with me at all times but I want it to be a branch of me not all me.

∞‡∞
Superstitions and Routines.

In top level sports they go through a physical routine, to get the body and mind as one to complete one specific task such as kick a rugby ball through a set of posts. The routine is designed to focus the mind away from the pressure of the situation and to physically do the same thing that works each time.

This is one thing and is related to superstition in part. A superstition, such as a lucky shirt, or putting the left sock on first may help a person not become distracted by worrying thoughts. However it can become a thing in itself. A person may go through a ridiculous routine and any deviation becomes a problem and takes your focus like those people who have to check the door is locked ten times, not nine, not eleven, ten.v Do not do this.

I found it much better to have no superstitions or routines but to get into character instead. Part of the character was to be above mere superstition and to laugh at it.

∞‡∞
Desire.

Your desire needs to be directed and mastered. If you have no desire for winning, for your martial arts, you will not progress quickly and you will reach a plateau. However, if your desire is unrealistic you will become frustrated and find a reason to give up. You will experience many people come to your club and say they want to fight professionally, they want to become world champions, people who cannot beat anyone at your club yet. This is a delusion and they are very likely to quickly give up when the delusion is shattered. Great is the humble person who just wants to learn.

∞‡∞
Small Thoughts – Big Ideas.

Sometimes a small thought appears in your mind. You should let this thought flourish and grow and see where it leads you. It maybe that it is something immediately useful but more often than not you put it aside only to come across it again at a later date when you can more fully understand it and develop it more.

Be proud of these thoughts, they are your children.

You can sometimes catch these half formed ideas from other people. They will tell you something, half embarrassed at their unformed thought. You may be able to catch it and complete it for them and learn something new together. Submission grappling is a two person activity after all.

∞‡∞
Mental Strength.

Mental strength is as important as physical strength. In many ways it can be judged of as a quantity in a similar way to physical strength, some people have more of it than others and it is obvious to everyone.

∞‡∞
Courage?

This is coloured in my mind by the idea of courage from WW1. Imagine being in the trenches in WW1, under constant bombardment for days, the sheer horror or what they saw, the debilitating constant fear and lack of rest. Then when they broke they were called coward. This is not what I want to talk on. I only feel able to talk about this in the following narrow way.

Cowardice, in terms of facing fear and the difference between dangerous showing off and courage. Some people do scary things. Young boys often run across factory roofs for fun and others decide not to do this. Are the ones on the roof brave and those who refuse cowards? Or are the people on the roof not brave because they do not see the danger. Are the people who refuse to go up brave for saying no?

To decide who is brave you will have to wait for an incident such as the following. You are in a group. One of your grouped is attacked. There is no doubt of the danger, everyone can see it. Who goes to their aid and who runs away? In my experience it is more likely the people who do not go on the roof.

∞✝∞
Psychopaths.

The strong simple way to introduce this is to remind you that some people are psychopaths.

You will come across people who are cruel. Some people get pleasure out of hurting other people. At extremes these people are aware of what they are and become devious to try to hide it. You should know these people. They will try to look for weaknesses in you, try to sow discord in your club so that they can operate as they wish under the cover of chaos. If you are invincible they will not challenge you because of course they are a form of coward at heart. If you have to confront them do it coldly. If they do not stop they have to leave.

Some people get pleasure, or do not seem to mind at least, getting hurt themselves. They smile as they talk to you about how their broken arm protruded from their skin. They look confused and then laugh as they see you have gone pale. If you remember when you were younger there were certain people who would do dangerous things to show off that you would never dream of doing. Some of those people grow out of it, some end up in prison and some dead. These people are not devious. They just need you to give them the boundary of other people for them because they do not know it themselves. If you have their respect they will take direction on this from you very happily and will not be offended. Devious people on the other hand are easily offended and you will literally be able to see in their eyes them planning their revenge on you.

∞✝∞
Fear.

Fear is of course a natural reaction. What is happening is your body is giving you a huge boost of energy and adrenalin to take the first and obvious solution to danger, which is to run away. Remember, this is the first option. If that option is not appropriate then you must master your fear, like taming a horse. If you can tame it, it will become a fantastic tool for you.

In my experience there are two types of fear, hot and cold. A hot fear is about a distant threat. Your worries build fear higher and higher, getting hotter. A hot fear makes you feel like your heart may explode. How you deal with this is simply to freeze your mind. It cannot be said in a simpler way than that. Let your mind bring your body under control, speak to yourself calmly and slowly.

A cold fear or a cold sweat is an instant fear. You have jumped to peak fear instantly, taking you cold. A cold fear is one where you feel you may faint. Let your body bring your mind out of this. What you need to do is warm up, move fast, act. When you are coming out of this cold fear you may even chose for yourself a more helpful mental state. Maybe it would be more helpful and appropriate to be angry for instance?

Your answer to a hot fear is mentally led; your answer to a cold fear is physically led. You are bringing your physical and mental sides closer together.

8 PRINCIPLES

1.   Do the opposite.
2.   Both ways.
3.   Crossing.
4.   Changing the order.
5.   Spotting new moves.
6.   Remove yourself.
7.   Break one part.
8.   Chaos.
9.   Change the position of your opponent's body.
10.   Car crash.
11.   Misalign the spine.
12.   Change of speed/direction.

PRINCIPLES.

When you have reached a high level you should look for general principles that can be applied in different situations. It is the general principle that is important. Look for these in successful places. If you can spot a general principle it will lead to new finishes, new escapes, a deeper understanding. It will give you the ability to beat opponents who are bigger, fitter, stronger. The following will possible give ideas to find them

∞✝∞
Do the opposite.

When you are trying to do something and not succeeding you may find success by doing the opposite of your intention. If you cannot move one way you may be able to go the opposite way. If holding isn't working, what would happen if you let go? If pulling isn't working, what would happen if you pushed? Instead of going forward, go back?

Doing the opposite is a good way of finding new ideas, new solutions. This is a very fruitful principle. In fact it has probably brought more success than anything else except the basics. It also leads into the next paragraph, both ways.

∞✝∞
Both ways.

It is good to have a number of options from one position. It is even better if some are in direct opposition to each other. For example, if your opponent has you in a hold down position, if you only have one escape one way, for example going away from him, your opponent can defend against it by over compensating his position against your move. If you have escapes both ways, away and towards him, once you make him move to defend one of your escapes he will make the other easier for you.

This is the same if you have finish options in both directions. If he resists your attack in one direction he propels himself in the opposite direction to your other finish.

If you have a pair of these you should think of them as one thing and be ready and waiting to go directly between them. It is even more beneficial if you have multiple methods.

∞✝∞
Crossing.

Crossing is when your opponent's arm or leg crosses his own body. If you can get beyond that arm or leg you can pin it down or strike the exposed side.

Crossing opportunities are looked for in all martial arts and submission grappling is no different. This is a general principle. You can create opportunities if you can induce your opponent to cross himself. If you have your opponent in a hold down, generally it is easier to bring a far limb towards you than to push a near limb away because your opponent does not recognise this as having the same vulnerability.

Like all moves they can be forced, snatched, tricked, set up or psychologically induced.

An example of the above is where you are across him with your chest to his chest pinning him down in side hold. What you do is turn your body towards his head on your side. If you are pointing towards his left arm you may put your left hand under his head and pull it forwards to secure him. Your attack is going to be on his left arm and it may be advantageous to put your right arm under his left arm, maybe holding under his upper arm. He will be tempted to bring his arms forward to push you away at your chest. What you do is let your left side drop back and push his left arm across you so that it goes under your left arm, you now turn and drop down. You have him in your hold with his arm trap across his body. He cannot bring his arm back because of your weight and you may launch an attack on that left side and he has no arm to defend it.

∞✝∞
Changing the order.

Position before submission is a foundational mantra. You cannot finish without a strong base position. Generally a submission follows the following three step order of first gain superior or hold down position; second, wrap up the target, e.g. an arm and then thirdly go for submission. This is how most moves are taught and how most people fight. You may find it fruitful to change the order of the first two, wrap up target first, e.g.

grab the arm, then move your body to hold down position, then go for your submission.

Let us say there is a finish on an arm where you have to have the opponent in a particular position. It is often possible to wrap the arm up in a different position you intend to finish on, and then take him to the required position second. For example, a particular arm lock may require the strength to do it from a top position but you have the opportunity to capture the arm while under your opponent. Once you have wrapped up the arm you may not be able to finish him but you may be able to force the arm enough to get him to reverse into the position you want and then finish him from there.

∞‡∞

Spotting New Moves.

You will find few people who develop new moves. You will see people come across a move by accident or an adaptation to a move. They will probably laugh about it like it was a freak of nature never to be repeated and then immediately put it out of their mind unaware that they are ignoring a possible whole new world of development.

Whenever you come across a strange new thing you should let your mind wander over it and gently question the fragile thing. You may not be able to do that for some time so you must plant a flag in your mind so that you can come back to it later. You will need to be so careful with it. Something new like this will be like picking up one thousand year old paper, just touching it can destroy it.

This you will find in more detail later in the section 'developing new moves.'

You should notice that putting wrap up target before position does not go against the major principle, position before submission.

∞‡∞

Remove yourself.

Sometimes it is advantageous to remove yourself. To remove yourself means to disengage in the current activity by moving far away from it, probably by a surprising and big movement. As a result of this you will be in a position that is neutral and equally advantageous to both you and your opponent.

It would be unproductive to leave an advantageous position so it is only done to leave a disadvantageous one, or a stalemate position. It could be that your opponent had the upper hand from a better position or is particularly adept at that position. Often he will be so engrossed in trying to dominate the position he will not see the possibility that you can disengage. When you do it will come as a surprise and a disappointment to him.

Two common instances of this are; firstly, when your opponent is on his back in open guard and you are trying to get to him and he is fighting you well with his arms and legs, you can remove yourself backwards out of his reach and then if you are quick you can go right around his legs towards his head and chest. Secondly you have your opponent in your guard between your legs and he has gone high. Rather than fight from your back, you can come up and quickly remove your legs from in front of you and get onto your feet into the start position again. You give up guard position, which is your legs wrapped around his waist. Neutral position is more positive than a negative position.

∞‡∞

Break one part.

Your opponent may be close to a finish on you. At this stage it may be impossible to break out of the whole move, but it may still be possible to stop the submission by unpicking one part of it. Look at how the move is constructed; is there a part of it that you can undo? A part that can be destroyed or even just held in check?

An example of this is the straight forward leg lock. Many people try to struggle their way out but find they cannot. One of the reasons for this is your opponent's foot pushed into your chest keeping you down. All you have to do is remove this foot and there is not enough power to finish you with the leg lock because the fulcrum for it is gone. Obviously you then have to act before he puts the foot back into your chest, but the principle is to destroy the finish by destroying one element of it.

∞‡∞

Chaos.

If your opponent is coming close to trapping you in a submission hold, one form of defence is to power up and throw yourself out. This is obvious and a natural instinct to everyone, but there are some important things to be aware of. As well as destroying your opponent's move by sheer power, you are also destroying it by making your movements chaotic for your opponent. He cannot put you back into his favoured position because of your power, yes, but also because he cannot keep track of your position, your movements.

There is also an important third element to your actions. Your movements must be chaotic to your opponent, but not to you. How you do this is the same as described before. You throw your move and then let it continue as you switch your concentration to how you are going to exit his trap and secure your position. While he is seeing chaos, you clearly see your escape.

∞‡∞
Change the position of your opponent's body.

Your opponent maybe attacking you with his arms and legs and making it difficult for you to get what you want. The straight forward solution is to try to win the fight of the arms and legs, but an alternative strategy is to force his body position to change. This stops the attack from his arms and legs at source and switches the fight to your favour.

One version of this is to straighten out your opponent. If you are on top of him and have him pinned he may try and scoot away from you by pushing with his arms and legs and try to get his waist back and away from you. If you have him pinned at the waist with one arm and your weight and also have your arm under his neck, instead of trying to fight his arms and legs you simply stretch his head away from his body. This stretch will flatten him down and stop him escaping. Also he will have to defend it or it will lead to a submission. When he tries to defend it you should be looking for opportunities to go for a finish move.

∞‡∞
Car crash.

You can utilise the car crash principle in many circumstances. If you are driving your car at sixty miles per hour and crash it into a parked car. However, if you are driving your car at the same speed and hit a car coming the other way; that is another.

There are many instances you can use this. If your opponent moves towards you you can move towards him and close the distance, taking him by surprise. If he is trying to force you over, or if he is trying to force your arm to move, you can resist him and then suddenly let go. All this induces the feeling in him you have when you expect there to be another step on the stairs and there is not.

Again, it is not just the speed that enables you to take advantage, it is the confusion. You may take the time to act, before he adjusts and gets his bearings again.

∞‡∞
Misaligning the spine.

If you have your opponent pinned down with your arm under his neck you can take away forty percent of his strength without him realising. What you do is you lean your shoulder into his jaw so that he take his head off centre line i.e. put his ear towards his shoulder. With his spine bent he will be fighting inefficiently. You must use your arm and shoulder in such a way that it is still uncomfortable for him in his present position but impossible and excruciatingly painful for him to try to straighten his spine. Physically he is distracted a little by the pain and a little confused, but psychologically he has chosen to accept this position as preferable to straightening his spine.

This is very important as when he fights, even though he is fighting at only sixty percent of his power, he thinks it is one hundred percent. Technically it a hundred percent in his new position which is only sixty percent of his best position. He will be in awe of your victory and unaware that he has been tricked. He will be aware of the pain in his jaw but he will not be aware of what the miss alignment of his spine has achieved for you.

You may be able to misalign his spine from other positions.

∞‡∞
Change of speed/direction.

Speed and direction may not be enough to beat your opponent. If you are in your car driving at eighty miles an hour you are comfortable and do not feel it. If you were to brake suddenly you would feel it even though you are slowing down. Changes of speed and direction are very important. You feel acceleration, you may not feel speed. Those who can work with changing rates of acceleration will gain great rewards.

9 TRAINING

1.   Warm ups.
2.   Stretching.
3.   Drilling.
4.   Remembering moves.
5.   Experimenting.
6.   Injuries.
7.   Clones.
8.   Handicapping.
9.   Too intense.
10.   Fighting fit.
11.   Exhaustion.
12.   Always a student.

TRAINING.

Warm ups.

Warm ups should be fun. They should develop fitness, flexibility, stamina, balance and coordination.

As I have got older I bother less and less with separate warm ups or stretching. I use quick warm ups with the specific intension of getting the body hot. The body adapts to what it does so I have my students warm up with light fighting (rolling), practicing hold downs and escapes or drilling basic moves. This develops fitness, stamina, balance and coordination specific to the requirements of submission grappling. The main reason for doing general warm ups is for the atmosphere in the club. It is a time for humour, camaraderie, welcoming new people, showing off what you all can do.

∞✝∞
Stretching.

Bearing in mind that I have moved away from separate warm ups, I also do not spend a lot of time developing separate stretching. However, I will sometimes run through a full yoga program. Yoga is excellent and perhaps we should all be doing that every day anyway. Those people who start yoga later in life all say they wished they had started it sooner.

∞✝∞
Drilling.

Drilling basic moves over and over is a wonderful thing and it enables you to enter flow.

∞✝∞
Remembering Moves.

Many people have trouble remembering moves. The brain works on connections so you can use this fact to help you.

On individual moves you can number each stage of a move and count it out as you train it. When you are first learning a move this will help you remember it. When you have used it a lot it will help you improve it by improving or changing the components.

Another thing you can do to help you is remember which positions lead to which submissions. You have the position in mind and the submissions radiate out from there.

∞╬∞
Experimenting.

It is okay to experiment against weaker opponents, but you will do both of you a favour if you point out finishes you are letting go along the way. Do not get trapped into admiring a complicated finish against a person you could have beaten in ten other ways. When you come to try your complicated finish under more extreme circumstances you may find yourself in great difficulty instead.

∞╬∞
Injuries.

There are two types of injuries. One type, that even though it can be frustrating and painful, you must train through. These are just muscle injuries. Your muscles are designed to work, tear and repair. If you train they will get stronger and other muscles will compensate. You may even find you are soon quickly, stronger and fitter.

This can even the case where your Doctor advises you not to train. Many people have quit exercising because they twisted an ankle and their Doctors advised them to quit sport. In this matter Doctors do not think this through. It is not as if people get fit and healthy by doing nothing, or that they are going to live forever. You must remember that your body needs to be used and will one day give up and take you with it. Your body is merely a tool to be used during your lifetime, but it should be considered a great gift and treasure.

The second type of injury is the type where you must rest and recover and this splits into many types. One is bad colds, flues and infections. The other is physical injuries that need time to repair, where you should not train, or train lightly. You must listen to your body and to experienced people at the club who have seen similar things before. Lastly, there are injuries that do truly threaten your ability to train permanently. These should be extremely rare. Accidents can happen to anyone anywhere, but it should not be because of errors and bad training methods at your club.

If you have any kind of injury or doubt you must inform your instructor and your training partners.

∞‡∞
Clones.

It is difficult for members of a club not to develop similarities in fighting; similarities without knowing that is what is happening. Having an open door policy is invaluable in keeping new ideas coming in to guard against this. A new comer may not have any new move to offer but will bring a new rhythm, new angles a new body language. A club that closes its doors to new ideas may last a thousand years but is in reality dead from that moment.

∞‡∞
Handicapping.

When a stronger fighter fights a much weaker fighter he can be handicapped in a number of ways. He may be required to only go for particular finishes only, such as leg locks only, or not allowed to use the same finish more than once. In this way both get to practice.

∞‡∞
Too intense.

You may get the sense that during training some or all students are fighting too intensely and not progressing. This needs fine judging. You may alter this on occasion to improve learning. You may have one student only defend and one only attack. You may have them fight one for one. This means that one student is allowed to find a finish and then it swaps to the other without one hundred percent resistance. This takes away the worry of losing. Students are initially unsure of this but after experiencing it they will come directly up to you afterwards and say how good it was and how much they enjoyed it. They can get into positions they would never usually get.

All students enjoy the pressure of trying to win taking off them on occasion.

∞‡∞
Fighting Fit.

In submission grappling you can say that new people lose. You can also say that experienced grapplers, if they are away for some time, do not come back immediately to their previous level. They have to regain their fitness and their feel for it. It is not the big moves that are the problem; it is the micro moves, sense and timing. In football they call this match fitness, but it is not just fitness.

∞‡∞
Exhaustion.

You should at times train to exhaustion, not just for the physical side, but the psychological side is extremely important in this. How you can test and train your students for this is to take them to exhaustion, pretend it is over and then ask them to continue. E.g. If they are continually fighting students one after another, tell them this is the last person, give them a moment and then ask them to fight on. This is how the special-forces train. Remember, though, you are teaching them, not breaking them.

∞‡∞
Always a student.

It is an obvious thing to think that you will always be learning so adopt the correct mind-set.

In ancient Japan everyone starting martial arts started with a new white belt. Over time the belt became darker and darker. A fighter could tell how experienced another fighter was by looking at the colour of their belt. The darker the belt, the more experienced the fighter. If you saw someone with a near black belt you knew you were in for a difficult time. I like the idea of this.

You will have older experienced members who no longer wish to fight intensely. These people can have great knowledge, be very helpful to new students and guide other students. You may come across a strange situation that is new and unique to you but they will have seen it before. These people are a treasure to your club.

10 ETIQUETTE

1. When to tap.
2. Harmony.
3. Giving all you know.
4. New students.
5. Aggression.
6. The main lesson.
7. Entertainment.
8. Consider your training partner.
9. Widen your learning.
10. Rules.

ETIQUETTE.

∞‡∞
When to tap?

You must always ensure you tap in time. You never know how long it will take to recover from injury, if you ever do, never the less, try not to tap too soon. Often you can be surprised at escaping a position you thought you would never escape from, or your opponent suddenly quitting, not knowing you were about to tap. You should know your own body and the temperament of your opponent. Be careful particularly with new people and people from other clubs who do not fully know or respect your club yet.

The role of your instructor is paramount in this.

∞‡∞
Harmony.

If you are running your own martial arts club it is essential that you ensure harmony. You must not tolerate anyone who goes against the harmony of the club. If someone causes problems you must neutralise them. Failing that you must get rid of them.

There are many ways to neutralise someone.

Humans are pack animals and every strong pack needs a leader whose position is unquestioned. You will need to make the correct use of fear to run your club. As Machiavelli said, you need to be feared but not hated or held in contempt. You need to fight off any attempts at usurping your authority. While there may be the odd occasion someone has to suffer your wrath, this is much more preferable to a club in disorder where everyone suffers all the time.

∞‡∞
Give all you know.

If you wish to get better, the best way to do it is to give all you know to as many people as possible. Whatever you give comes back to you many times over. This is a difficult concept to grasp and we are all tempted to hang onto our little tricks and secrets. We worry that if we tell our opponent how we beat them then we won't be able to defeat them next time.

Firstly we all have our debts to pay. If you know a thousand things about grappling you will be lucky to claim to have discovered two things on your own, both of which someone else has probably already discovered as well. We all had teachers and it is not down to us to pretend we did not and to break the chain.

Even if the above were not true, it is a good thing in itself anyway. Every time you give all you know, the next time you train there will be something new there waiting for you. It maybe something completely new or an old thing in a new way. Every time you hold onto something it will be there waiting as your self-imposed limit the next time you train and each time it will be harder to keep it secret. When you tell all and think there will be nothing left something new appears on the horizon and it is a wonderful thing. Again, the natural temptation is to grasp it close as a secret.

You can also be only so far ahead of everybody else, just a little better. In limiting the education of those around you, you ultimately limit your own education. Acting in this way is the best way to ensure harmony in your club, you encourage the idea of generosity and giving, not secrecy.

∞╪∞
New Students.

Of the hundreds of new arrivals you will fight or watch fight you will see that the story is practically identical every time. The new person fights hard and fast and clings on. The trained fighter is far more controlled and quietly works to a win. The situation is repeated so that the beginner has a half position, classically gripping the experienced person's wrists when he stops and says, "I don't know what to do now".

Most men think they can fight. It is important to them. They have grown up reading books and watching films of fights and fighters. In their day dreams they are heroes and no matter what the odds against them they come out on top. If someone breaks into their house and threatens their wife and children, they will step up and save the day. Most people never actually fight beyond childish fights. How can they be good at it?

If you are training to a high standard you will fight policemen and members of the armed forces and beat them with ease. This should both make you proud of the skills you have learned but in a wider sense should concern you. These people are protectors of the public and are the very people who should know how to fight.

∞✝∞
Aggression.

You will learn to control and direct your aggression at a good club. With experience you should get to the stage where someone can be very aggressive, trying to intimidate you and you can remain calm and unaffected.

∞✝∞
The main lesson.

The main lesson in martial arts is the same as in all life. You should aim for dignity in all things.

∞✝∞
Entertainment.

Young school pupils can cause trouble for their own entertainment by asking two older boys which of them is the toughest. At a club there are some weak fighters who for their own entertainment ask two great fighters who is the better fighter. This reflects very poorly on them. If this is you and you are considering this you need to think twice as you are liable to receive an instant invitation you are likely to have to humiliatingly decline.

∞✝∞
Consider your training partner.

You should have consideration for your training partner. As well as some people being naturally selfish there is also a scientific fact. If you give another person pain you always underestimate how much it hurts them. In other words if two people fight equally hard, each think the other person is being rougher than they are themselves being. This can lead to them mistrusting each other or falling out if they are unaware of this.

∞✝∞
Widen your learning.

When you have reached a particular level you should experience different instructors, otherwise, how are you going to beat the person who has taught you everything you know? Your instructor should be understanding about this. It will make him better when you bring your new knowledge back.

∞‡∞
Rules.

Submission grappling is a martial art and a sport, as such fighters fight to rules. Different clubs and different competitions have different rules. Rules mean a number of things; firstly different rules mean different fights. Under some rules you will make certain techniques work, but if the rules change they may not be effective or appropriate. Different rules may even mean different fighters win. Think clay court or grass court in tennis.

Secondly, anyone who has ever entered a martial arts contest has spent most of their time before and after talking about rules because they are so important to the fight. It is a sad situation but the fighter who adapts best to the rules greatly improves his chance of winning the contest. You need to be aware of this for your competition fighting, but more so if you ever fight for real. If you are in a very restrictive martial art, such as no holding, no fighting on the floor, then you might not do as well as you think in a real fight were your opponent does not restrict themselves to these rules.

11 TEACHERS

1. Leadership.
2. What do you feel?
3. Fighter or teacher?
4. Knowledge.
5. Practice.
6. Wider view.

TEACHERS.

∞✝∞
Leadership.

A leader inspires those around him with the pure joy of living and the preciousness of human life.

∞✝∞
What do you feel?

You need great teachers but more and more you need to listen to your own voice in parallel to all the other voices trying to guide you. If you don't, you will stagnate, you will not develop to your highest possible level. If you feel something to be true, or even have the merest feeling for something you must push on through and test it, think about it. Sometimes it may even take years and countless examples before you believe what you have been feeling and not quite believing. Do not be overly harsh with yourself about this, but vow to yourself to be more confident in your own judgement in future.

∞✝∞
Fighter or Teacher?

It has been heard said that there is a difference between a fighter and a teacher and that you cannot be a good teacher until you give up fighting. This needs a lot of thought.

Maybe it is not so simple and straight forward as the saying goes. While you will find many good fighters are indeed selfish and unable to teach, those who teach submission grappling also need to be very good fighters. Even if a teacher has a wider repertoire than his student, if the student can beat his teacher he will quickly become disillusioned with him.

All teachers of any kind, school or parents know that there is an alternative and that is distraction. In martial arts this means ruling by badges, belts, and other forms of idolatry. Meanwhile you do not learn anything of value. This is the route of the charlatan. You will find it very difficult not to be taken in. You need to ask the following questions. Is what I am taught useful? Does it work? Am I making progress? Do I get to fight people who are better than me to learn from experience or am I fighting someone the same as me all the time? Is my instructor hiding in plain sight in front of me and I never get to practice with him? What is he doing if he is not fighting? Is he stood there, hands on hips looking stern and shouting instructions, telling you that you are not doing things right hand he comes and makes some little adjustment to what you are doing that makes no sense to you?

∞‡∞
Knowledge.

There is no substitute for practicing under the tutelage of a great teacher, but you can learn from books, videos, dvds, the internet to add to your knowledge.

As well as practicing for real with a partner, it is beneficial to learn in the following ways;

Running through moves in your mind when you can find a peaceful moment (in bed before you fall asleep at night is a good time). This is an excellent method for sharpening up your technique. The more real and vivid you can imagine it the better.

Explaining it to someone else, becoming a teacher. As you try to explain it to someone else you understand it better yourself. You may find that you cannot explain a move you can do and have to go to your instructor for help in explaining it. This will show you that there is a gap in your understanding and you will listen and learn yourself.

∞‡∞
Practice.

While teaching helps you develop your technique, there is no substitute for practice. If you have spent any time instructing, even one session, you will become aware of this. You are aware that you have not had that physical adrenalin burst that you are used to. You are also aware that students who are practicing hard will be closing the gap to you and will be able to beat you eventually if you do not get your own practice in.

You need to be aware of this as the chief instructor. Many fighters can be selfish and only want to train. They do not wish to spend their training time helping weaker members learn. This can mean that the burden of instructing falls only to certain people and although they do not mind this and enjoy it, their own progress may slow. It is your job as an instructor to make sure that this burden is shared and if possible all students are aware of their responsibilities in this area. At times you may have to shun a selfish student and spend more time with those who have given their time to the group rather than just themselves.

This is something that needs to be understood. You may be tempted to let the situation develop as in the short term it may benefit you as your teaching time is shared, but if a selfish student gets good quickly without helping others he will become arrogant and think he has done everything himself, not seeing what others have sacrificed for him.

∞‡∞

Wider view.

If you are teaching you will need to use your position as a strength, to improve your own learning. While you will miss out on some practice through teaching your position enables a wider view. You can see this in professional sports when a competitor gets injured and unable to practice for a length of time. They often spend their time watching from the side lines and when they come back from injury they come back with new insights they would not have found otherwise. It is a fact that many good football managers are ex-footballers who had to quit their career early through injury. This need pondering.

Training all the time, competing can narrow your focus, which is good, but we all benefit from stepping back from time to time.

12 GENERAL

1.   Calmness.
2.   Letting go.
3.   Reactions.
4.   Animals
5.   A living thing.
6.   Number two.
7.   An interesting case.
8.   General thought.
9.   Experiences.
10.   Belief.
11.   Delusions.
12.   Two good fighters.

GENERAL.

∞✝∞
Calmness.

While most people new to the sport cannot help throwing everything in and thrashing around blindly, you need to curb this as soon as possible. I have found that some opponents keep a habit of fidgeting, rocking back and forth in a position rather than keeping still, even switching complete hold down positions without making any attempt to win in the first hold down position. Invariably this habit is picked up from kick-boxing or boxing where it is advantageous to be constantly on the move to give and to avoid strikes.

In submission grappling this jerky movement will not be helpful. You will not be able to exert as much pressure on your opponent as your movements will constantly relieve the pressure, but most importantly, you will take away your own senses.

If you rock back and forth, this movement can only come from brain signals. You are giving your brain a job to do, send those signals. You are also making it harder to do your task which is to look at your opponent, analyse the situation and look for opportunities to win. It will be harder because you are having to adjust to this from a constantly moving position. In kick-boxing or boxing this will also give an equal problem. It would be better to keep still, apart from, of course, the fact that they can strike you and win the fight, which trumps everything else. If you are grappling and you have hold of your opponent and they cannot strike you then you do not need to counter something that they cannot do.

∞✝∞
Letting go.

In submission grappling one of the most important things is to let go. If your opponent grips hold of you, unless it is purposefully, that is only good news for you. That hand helps you to understand his body position and what you need to do. It is a hand but because it is gripping, is not able to do anything else and your hands are free.

When people first start they cling onto you gripping with all their might and think they are doing alright. They do not notice your organised movements that alter your position to a dominant position so that you can get to a submission. It seems to come from nowhere for them. It takes a long time to learn what a useful hold is and what is not. Some fighters never fully learn this, what is good holding on and what is just occupying your mind. They do not progress as they should.

When people first start they often only last a few minutes before they blow out, yet trained fighters can train for hours. Part of the answer is getting fitter, but most of it is learning to let go and fight efficiently.

Sometimes a new student will stop part way though and say. "I don't know what to do", which is an awaking for them. How they progress or if they never turn up again depends on how they answer it for themselves. Yes they have realised it is like a chess game and moves, counter moves need to be learned. They have seen the journey they need to make. Whether they are prepared to make that journey is a different story. Some just do not want to make the effort. For other people, ego is the problem. Many men think that being able to fight is manly and natural. They presume, without any evidence to support it, that they will be able fighters, able to defend their women and families when to an able experienced fighter, they are but dust.

∞‡∞
Reactions.

Different martial arts react in different ways. I was first taught jiu-jitsu. When attacked you stepped forward to grab and or strike your opponent. I did not realise this was the case until I went to a karate class, where I would step forward, they stepped back. Whereas I had been trained to grab my opponent; that was exactly what they had been trained to avoid, to step away.

In submission grappling this moving in is even more the case. In all previous martial arts they train to instantly react when someone grabs hold of you, to jump, flinch and fight. They train to have a hair trigger response. After years of submission grappling I have completely evolved the other way. I do not flinch when someone grabs hold of me. I do not react to noise. My focus does not narrow, it widens.

When someone grabs hold of me, if I flinch I will lose all my senses. When someone grabs hold of me my focus clears. I can feel how strong they are. I can feel what they are about to do. Maybe pull me, try to hit me. By keeping my focus clear I can react correctly.

∞‡∞
Animals.

Man has always looked to the animal kingdom for ideas of fighting. A hyena gets a bigger prey to move and then follows it around, gives it little injuries if it can, waits for it to tire and then attacks. A snake hides from its prey and launches a single deadly strike. A mongoose grapples a snake to submission. A spider makes an invisible trap. A falcon drops from hundreds of feet and strikes. Some animals don't attack and simply defend until the predator gives up. A fox has many ways to escape and this can be effective. A cat is not as clever and may just run up the nearest tree and that can be effective. To human beings many animal powers seem like superpowers but we are the top predator because we are the cleverest.

∞‡∞
A living thing.

When you get to a high standard it becomes a living, giving thing. All the very greatest fighters I have known have been humble, prepared to give all they know.

I have seen young, frustrated, aggressive, disrespectful people become calm, loyal, respectful students. I have seen trust and respect develop; lives led, stories told, a kind of comrades in arms.

I had a visitor, a poor man who had been attacked, beaten and robbed by three men. His whole family came as frightened rabbits, wife, son and daughter to support him. They wanted their life back, to feel free, to be able to walk the street without fear. I can do that for this man because of what I know.

∞‡∞
Number two.

As a leader of a club the best thing you can have is a totally loyal number two. If you have one loyal person in your club whose natural reaction is to support and advise you your club will be solid. If you do not have this then your club can succumb to factions and negativity.

∞‡∞
An interesting case.

I am going to describe a case that would be interesting in itself, but it has become even more interesting as I have seen a similar thing in more than one person now. In submission grappling the use of the hands are extremely important. As I have already described it is difficult to learn to let go but I have come across people with the opposite problem, never gripping hold.

Two cases of the same thing become even more interesting than one. While having some differences they had a great deal in common. Both of them held their hands in a solid cup shape and pushed and held their opponent with these cups (the back of their hands) or their wrists, even pushing at their chest with the back of their wrist like men who have had their hands cut off. It was as if their mind was not aware of their fingers as fingers. Obviously this limited their ability and their chance of success. Neither of them was aware of their problem until I pointed it out and even when I repeatedly pointed it out, both had great difficulty in dropping the technique and thinking of their fingers.

I do not know the cause of this. Maybe they had done some activity when they were younger where it was necessary to do this? Was it an activity where the fingers had to be protected? I do not know. It was a very strange thing.

∞‡∞
General thought.

Martial arts should not dominate your life to the extent that you have nothing else. It should enrich your life and the rest of your life should enrich your martial arts.

∞‡∞
Experiences.

Submission grappling is only one aspect of martial arts. You should experience other martial arts. Of particular use are all forms of ju-jitsu, boxing, kick-boxing, judo and wrestling. To be a good fighter you will need all round skills. If you are not interested in this and are just enjoying a sport, you should still experience other martial arts, sports, dancing, yoga etc. You will be surprised how it will open your mind and make you better at want you want to be. You will find it will enhance your knowledge of movement and how your body occupies space. Remember Bruce Lee was a world champion ballroom dancer.

∞✝∞
Belief.

You need to develop your ability to such an extent that your opponents lack the belief that they can beat you.

If you can do this you will notice your students split into two groups. The largest group will automatically not even count their results against you. They may say "I didn't get beaten today", and another student will think about it for a moment and then ask about him fighting you and he will say, "Oh I obviously don't count him".

There will be a much smaller group, maybe one student at any one time, who you will catch staring at you. You will clearly see their frustration and desire to win you all over their face. When you catch them starring they will jump a little as if caught steeling. You must laugh at them and tell everyone what they are doing, but in such a way that makes a joke of it. They will freely admit that beating you is their desire, their sole aim. Saying it out loud will make sure that it doesn't become a secret for them and make them angry and resentful. It also tells them that you know; you are the leader of the pack, because only the leader of the pack could get away with openly talking about it, knowing there will be the fight next time. Their losses will continue while your desire remains.

If you are very uncomfortable with the idea of someone targeting you like this, or someone coming through the door and challenging you, you need to step aside as fight leader.

∞✝∞
Delusions.

It never fails to surprise me how deluded some people are. I have tapped a new comer twenty times straight out and at the end they have started to give me their advice on what I should do. In submission grappling these people stand out straight away. Even so this delusion can continue for some time until the weight of their losses piles up and becomes undefendable even for them. Still, once afflicted, a person is liable to drift back into this habit.

For your own part, you must resist the urge to show off. No good will come of it. There is a difference between showing off and talking clearly and honestly about your ability. You will find people are unhappy with one and happy and accepting of the other.

∞‡∞
Two good fighters.

Often, when two good fighters come together who respect one another they do not fight full fights to a submission. They fight sections of fights and swap ideas and give each other what they know. Both gain from this. Other wise they can end up fighting to a stalemate and fighting the same fight over and over again, neither over committing and risking going down a new path. There is respect and honour in this.

13 REAL FIGHTS

1.   Consequences.
2.   General facts.
3.   Would you act?
4.   Time.
5.   Avoid them.
6.   Chaotic.
7.   Listen.
8.   What would happen if?
9.   The Law.
10.   First strike.
11.   Blocking – The fence.
12.   Set up – Physical.
13.   Set up – Psychological.
14.   Set up – Successful Strikes.
15.   Multiple opponents - Escape.
16.   Multiple opponents - Preparation.
17.   Multiple opponents - Information.
18.   Multiple opponents - Tactics.
19.   Martial arts that work.

REAL FIGHTS.

This section moves away from purely submission grappling but it is something we work on at the club because of its importance.

Consequences.

In school gyms there are those wooden benches. If you had to walk across it for a pound you would take that bet, but would you if the bench was between two high buildings? Suddenly it is not such an easy task, even though it is the same task. It is exactly the same task but the consequences are very different.

It is the same in fighting. All those ideas you have, all those beliefs are suddenly called into question when it becomes a real fight. This is true psychologically and physically. You will be like the little old lady shouting instructions to the heavy weight boxer in the twelfth round. Why doesn't he just do this or that, it's easy. All it takes is for you to be punched hard in the head once for you to understand.

∞‡∞
General Facts.

Ninety nine percent of fighting is mere skirmishes. There may be some shouting and bravado, even some pushing and shoving and that will be it. Even if it gets to punches being thrown, in the majority of cases one person throws a punch or two while the other cowers from them. Within twenty seconds they are then out of sight of each other. The puncher is happy because he can pretend he is a big brave hard hero and the punched is happy that it wasn't any worse than it was.

If both people fight, which is very rare, it will not be anything like boxing or television fights where they stand and swap punches. After a couple of punches they will be grabbing one another to stop being punched because it hurts so much. In the following melee they will in all likelihood end up on the floor and become exhausted in thirty seconds to two minutes. The adrenalin that is pumping through them will mean they are unaware of most of their injuries and what is going on around them. They will be shocked at how exhausted they are. They will be shocked at being so close to another human being, their breathing, their smell will seem animal like to them. They will rest, holding onto each other between burst of activity where they maybe too exhausted to hurt each other. They will realise that they don't really know how to fight and are relieved that the other person doesn't either. They will gradually become more aware of their surroundings and the future consequences of what has happened or may still happen. Both will want to be away and at the first opportunity the fighters will almost certainly part. Unless there is a serious injury their energies will then be spent trying to repair their pride.

Afterwards they may talk about the punches they did not feel but the thing that will haunt them and make them think that they never want to fight again will be the exhaustion and the combined idea that they did not know what to do and were too exhausted to do it. It will frighten them because it felt like the approach of death and they will not talk about that part.

∞╪∞
Would you act?

Would you respond? You may be surprised when you come face to face with it. You may think, if my family is attacked I would gain supper strength and fight anyone and everyone. The truth is that you may be too shocked and stunned. It may be over so quickly that you find you have done nothing. Alternatively you may think you would be a coward and do nothing and yet afterwards find that you have rushed into a dangerous situation without care of the consequences.

∞╪∞
Time.

There is often a time factor involved in fights.

Instant fights. There is nothing you can do about preparing for it, you are involved. You must do your best to instantly adjust and not freeze. Under the right circumstances we are all heroes and all cowards. You might think you are prepared but if the situation or timing is different to what you are expecting you may find yourself lost. What you need to do is bring the mind set back you had. Harden and freeze your mind and your body will unfreeze.

Medium - e.g. you are in a night club and have an altercation. The person or group is still on the premises and may be brooding over it and winding themselves/each other up to fight. You need to make a tactical decision, probably to leave. In this country there are such strong social etiquettes to avoid embarrassment. If you are in danger you need to see through these, think clearly and act.

Long term – the build-up of long term disputes and feuds. Here the danger is pride. People have an over blown sense of their own importance and intellect. The things that they do that annoy the opposite party are felt unimportant, but what the opposite party does to you is over blown. Move on and get over it. Even if it does come to blows it will not be good for your health. Literally, move on if necessary. I have heard so many people say 'Move? Why should I move, I've done nothing wrong? Let him move'. Meanwhile their blood pressure rises, they are miserable and their time is spent in this state.

∞‡∞

Avoid them.

If at all possible you should do your best to avoid fighting for real. Real fights are dangerous in so many ways. This means avoiding the wrong place, wrong time and the wrong people. Many people feel they would like to fight for some reason, to test themselves. This is particularly the case with people who have trained in some form of martial arts. They want to see how good they really are. Some people have had this feeling for many many years and try to cover their desire in sugar for themselves.

"If someone tried to rob me I would…".

"If someone hurt my girlfriend…".

"He didn't do that to you did he? I'll sort it out for you..".

"I was in the taxi rank minding my own business when this idiot started on his girlfriend..".

You can always find an excuse for fighting, but apart from the danger to yourself, do you really want to take another man's life? How do you know it will not go that far once it starts? Everyone is interested in finding out what happened in a real fight, but if you have ever been in one, can you see any glory in it?

Everything in our society is geared to stop people fighting and this is only increasingly so. This was not always the case. There are also many places in the world where it is not the case. People are not encouraged in this country to settle their disputes by fighting. If you try you will find that society will act very strongly to discourage you either by direct punishments or indirectly by excluding you from many things. E.g. If you get a criminal record there will be many jobs that you will not be able to successfully apply for.

∞‡∞
Chaotic.

Real fights are chaotic and fast so do not be surprised and shocked. Look for control and opportunities to use your techniques.

∞‡∞
Listen.

You must listen to descriptions of real fights with great care. Thankfully they are rare, but because they are different to your training sessions you need to find facts on them whenever you can.

Half of what you will hear will be the physical part of the fight, the other half will be the emotional side of the fight. You will be surprised at how much the emotional side interferes with the physical. You will probably find yourself looking at someone who is great in training and always relaxed and you are taken aback at how shaken up they are from what was probably just a little skirmish. In the fight you must first master yourself emotionally before mastering your opponent physically. To help you do this tune into people who are naturally good at this and switch off to people who are poor at this. This is a great help. You should also be able to spot someone who tells lies about this subject, and shun then.

∞‡∞
What would happen if..?

Many people come to the club and ask this and that about fighting. 'What would happen if', and they are really concerned about being involved in a fight. You do not need to worry about this. It is very rare that you will get in a fight unless you are one of two types of people, over aggressive or over timid.

You may meet over aggressive people, who say they do not know why they end up in fights and then say to people in a public place, "What do you think you're looking at"? in an aggressive way to anyone who looks at them. Over timid people cower when spoken to and invite aggressive people to bully them.

You should never worry about being in a fight, you probably never will be. You should carry yourself with confidence but not aggression; otherwise it will come back to you. If you show confidence you are very likely to be left alone. If you train well, you should be calm and confident as one goes with the other.

∞‡∞
The Law.

In this modern world, people are concerned that the law will not protect them. They are concerned that even if they do not start a fight and are not to blame, they worry that they will be the one the police prosecute. This is particularly the case if they have been trained to fight in any way. They worry this will count against them. You should not worry about this. How long has the law been around? A few hundred years. How long has fighting been around? An infinite amount of time. Your first objective is to protect yourself and yours. Stay alive, win the fight and face your day in court if you have to.

It may be difficult for people sat in nice comfy seats in great safety to understand the situation you found yourself in and the decisions you made then. That may be a new fight you will have to face to convince them, but each fight in its own time.

You will be prosecuted, rightly, if you use excessive force. People who use excessive force have done so because they lose control, so stay in control.

∞‡∞
First strike.

You need to develop powerful set strikes, punches, kicks, knees and elbows. If you can win a fight quick and clean it benefits everyone. If the fight is unavoidable there is no stain on your character to strike first. Waiting to be hit first is ridiculous. You may be knocked unconscious and kicked to death. If you are fighting more than one opponent you will want to use strikes rather than grappling. If you become entangled with one the other is free to attack you.

∞╪∞
Blocking – The fence.

This is a well-developed tactic now. You can see it being used on the rugby field where the person with the ball uses it to fend off a tackler. You do not let your opponent near you by keeping a straight arm out to block and hinder his movement forward. Timing of putting your hand out is crucial. If you put it out too soon he will knock it away. If you put it out too late you will not be able to lock your elbow and he will continue forward. He should be stopped in his tracks.

This move stops him getting close to you to grab you and limits his ability to punch or kick you. Importantly you can feel his intentions and movements through your arm. When you block his movement you get the opportunity to speak to him, confuse him, placate him, or threaten him, whatever you think is appropriate.

This arm also enables you to set him up for your own strike. If he continues to come threatening forward you can let your arm give way and strike him.

∞╪∞
Set up - Physical.

Fighting is not just strength and chance. You can maximise your chance of winning by various techniques. Probably the most important, after developing your strikes, is the set up. You manoeuvre your own body, without your opponent being aware, to maximise your ability to strike freely and also for them not to be able to do so for you.

A simple example of this is a punch with your right arm. For power you need to draw your right arm far back and swing. If you turn your body subtly so that your right shoulder is farthest away from your opponent, this has drawn back your arm and all you have to do now is the punch forward part, making your attack quicker and much more likely to succeed. If you are going to swing a kick with your right leg, turn your right hip away subtly first.

Good street fighters will try to do this to you. If he looks like he is setting you up to swing an arm or a leg, move your position so that he cannot do so, he cannot gain this advantage over you. Do not wait. Do not worry about social conventions. Use the fence or some other way of stopping him entering striking distance to you. Remember you may strike first if necessary.

∞✝∞
Set up - Psychological.

They may try to intimidate you with actions, posture and words to keep you still like a frightened rabbit while they manoeuvre to set you up with a strike. You have to mentally fight this off and get control over yourself. If they see that you are not intimidated it will either completely stop them or if not it will slow or alter their attack.

Do not be fooled by a sudden change to friendly words and offers of hand shakes or pats on your back. This is particularly the case after an initial altercation. He maybe just trying to get close to you to get a cheap strike on you. Your best strategy is to speak calmly and tell him you accept his words but at the same time you keep him at arm's length. If he tries to come close to put his hands on you in a supposed friendly way you do not let him. Be firm on this. If you let him in physically he may not do an assault on you however he may walk away and start to think on it. He realises he is still angry with you. He feels his pride hurt and he is emboldened that you are weak. Without realising it you have been the catalyst of a future attack on you.

∞✝∞
Set up - Successful Strikes.

There are two halves to a strike. What comes from the blow, the angle, power etc and how the target is. Half of your set up is hitting the weak part you want to hit, jaw, nose, solar plexus, loins etc. The other half is hitting it to maximum purpose.

For example, there is a big difference being hit in the stomach when you are prepared for it and when you are not. This is the other half of the set up, to either strike when his body is unprepared to be hit or if you psych him out, he will leave it unprepared. Remember, that is what your opponent is trying to do to you.

The Kray twins had a method of setting people up. They offered them a cigarette and then offered to light it. The victim was either psyched out because it was the Krays or relaxed and concentrating on the cigarette. Mentally they were unprepared to be hit. Physically they were unprepared to be hit. Their jaw would be relaxed, vulnerable and open. The Krays would offer a match with one hand, would have their body turned and primed to punch them with the other. They knew how to punch as they were both boxers. More often than not they broke the victims jaw and knocked them out.

∞┼∞
Multiple opponents - Escape.

Book your escape route. With multiple opponents it is essential that you analyse the situation. Is there an escape route that you can take immediately or one you can work towards? A group can feel safe in numbers and encourage each other to fight. One member can also let his psychotic side out because he has an audience to show off to and although he might do something disgusting he knows the others have to share the responsibility with him. Your best bet is to get away and the quicker the better.

∞┼∞
Multiple opponents - Preparation.

You need to develop your striking capability. To win a fight you need some simple very effective techniques e.g. a great punch to jaw or stomach, a strong kick to knee or groin are best because you can keep your distance, strike and keep clear. You do not want someone clinging onto you while the others jump you.

Of secondary value are elbow and knee strikes, a devastating throw or a slam because you have to get closer to your opponent to make them work, but they can be extremely effective.

∞┼∞
Multiple opponents - Information.

You have to take in a lot of information very quickly.

What is their ability, size and weight?
How aggressive are they? How likely to fight are they? Have they been drinking? Can you rank them in terms of danger to you?
What is the ground like? Is it slippy? Is it hard? Is there anything that you can use for cover, for a weapon? How are they likely to use the ground?
What is your own status? What foot ware do you have on, clothes? Have you been drinking?
Do you have anything or anyone to protect? Can this person keep up with you if you run? Do they have anything or anyone to protect?

Do they know you? Do they know where you live? Do you know them or where they live?

∞‡∞

Multiple opponents - Tactics.

If you can not escape;

Going to ground. It is imperative that you avoid going down to the ground. If fights go on for any length of time they go to clinching standing up and then go down to the ground. You do not just fight to win; you have to fight to stay on your feet. If you go to ground you could literally end up dead. Your quieter opponents will suddenly get brave and step forward and kick you in the head for some of the glory and any idiot can kick you in the head. If you do go down you must not curl up to defend yourself, forget that, and fight with everything you have got to get back on your feet. Again, if you go down, you are finished.

Who to strike first? Part of your analysis must go into whom to strike first. This may be the nearest person. It might be the most aggressive. It might be the weakest. It might be the person blocking your escape route. It maybe someone you have chosen for other tactical reasons.

Try to fight one by one. You might be able to move so that your opponents end up in line one behind the other.

Hostages. You may be able to use your first victim as a shield to block the approach of others.

The use of viciousness. All those things that you are not supposed to do. To do them will take careful thinking but instantaneous thinking. If you are extremely vicious to the person you attack first e.g. kicking them in the knee cap, their loins, being vicious to their face, gauging, ripping their nose, continuing to strike the first one after he has been subdued; this may give you the opportunity to escape through their shock, horror or cowardice. It may make them realise the error of their ways and start to talk about stopping and taking their friend with them. Fighting was bravado and fun. Now it is suddenly serious and dangerous. People who start fights think they are going to win. They do not start fights thinking they are going to get hurt. You may however risk enraging them, making bystanders join in and also risk an escalation in what would have happened.

∞‡∞

95

Martial arts that work.

Mixed martial arts, boxing, kick boxing, good judo, good wrestling. People who have trained well in these will make a mess of you if you are untrained.

14 DEVELOPING NEW MOVES

1.   There is always a solution.
2.   Using a general principle from one area in a new area.
3.   Find new combinations.
4.   Knowledge of these principles.
5.   Detail and the whole picture.
6.   Desire
7.   Belief: There is always a solution.
8.   An open mind.
9.   Think about it.
10.   If necessary, drop it.
11.   Nurture it.
12.   When a new route stares you in the face.
13.   General.

DEVELOPING NEW MOVES.

∞╪∞
There is always a solution.

There is always a solution, the problem is finding it. Your first task is to search your mind, your senses for recognition of the current situation and the solution that flow from your memory of similar situations. If there is not one there you will have to discover one, invent a solution.

This may never occur to some people. They imagine there is a 'great book' written somewhere of every technique that is possible and if it is not in the book it is not possible. What they do not appreciate is that every technique started with someone in a situation and they discovered a technique to deal with it. This book it about methods to help you find those techniques when there is nothing in the book you have been given to deal with the situation you are faced with.

There is always a simple physical solution and if you do not know what it is your first step to finding it is to overcome the mental block that says it is impossible to find a solution and believe that there will be one. When you do eventually find it, it will be like a fog clearing with the solution obvious and staring at you from the start. You may find yourself laughing and thinking how ridiculous you could not see it before. You will think yourself simple for believing it was impossible.

In your development you will use known moves only. You will ask your instructors, read books, look at dvds, look on the internet for these moves. You will think that these are the only sources and for you they will be because you cannot invent without a depth of knowledge.

Your first awareness that you may be able to discover a move will be when you realise that to make a move work for you that you have been taught you have to make a slight adjustment to it. I have been through this and I have seen many students go through this. They call me across to discuss what they have done as if they have done something wrong and that they should not really be doing it that way even though the evidence of their own experience shows them that their adaptation works. I ask them, 'Did it work,' and they say, 'Well, yes.' And I say, 'Then it must be right then.'

Many students reject stepping over the line of their own experience and fall back to only doing it the way they have been told. A good instructor will develop the atmosphere in the club and individual students to go past this stage. In a poor club an insecure instructor will not welcome questions of this nature.

If you set your mind to not losing, to be determined to find a way and combine that with an open mind, you should find a way. You can encourage this by giving responsibility. When you are desperate, when you have to do it, you suddenly find a way. The following principles may give you a starting point.

∞✝∞
Using a general principle from one area in a new area.

When a move is successful; look at the element(s) that made it successful. It will be a general principle. All moves are based on physical principles that follow nature's laws. Try to find the general principle.

In a new situation, when you are struggling to find a breakthrough, go through your list of general principles. Will sacrifice work, what about taking his base, breaking one part, using a lever, using reversal, putting pressure on his neck, doing the opposite……

Your mind should quickly test if this principle is useful or not, to use or reject it and move onto the next principle.

Remember there is always a solution.

∞✝∞
Find new combinations.

A new move will often come from combining existing principles in new ways. Combining two or more existing ideas and principles into a new form. Sometimes this happens in the conscious where you physically see the combinations and make it work. Sometimes it materialises from the subconscious and you have done it before fully realising. You may have to turn detective to recreate it.

∞✝∞
Knowledge of these principles.

A conscious knowledge of these principles will aid you greatly. Bring them to the forefront of your mind.

∞‡∞
Details and the whole picture.

Look at details and the whole picture and swap between the two. Some people only look at details. While they can become exceptional at certain moves they are limited in their creative ability. People who look at the whole can appear more sloppy because they are weaker on knowing the detail, but they have an advantage over those who only concentrate on detail. If you can swap between the two you will have the advantages of both. People who can do this easily are rare.

∞‡∞
Desire.

If you do not have a desire to learn, to win and have a hatred of losing you will forever step back from breaking through. When you are faced with losing you will take it, you will not spend the next few weeks turning it over in your mind looking for a solution. When you have the first inclining of a new idea you will happily let it go. When you have your first criticism you will fold.

∞‡∞
Belief: There is always a solution.

Belief and desire are separate but related. You may desire to be a great fighter but lack belief. You may believe you are destined to be a great fighter but lack the desire to work at it.

To be a great fighter you will need the belief that, although you may not know it at the present instant, there is always a solution that can be found and you will need the desire to find it. This is most easy when you just set it like an automatic setting so that as soon as you come across a problem you immediately set your mind to find the solution.

There is also a very big physical element to submission grappling. You will need the belief that, although you cannot go on forever, you can always take one more step. Rather than again trying to bring desire in with a great big fanfare and putting yourself under enormous pressure all the time, set this extra step as an automatic thing. You should call the gods, your ancestors and your very soul only when you are truly desperate.

∞†∞
An open mind.

There needs to be a part of your mind open to new ideas. Only a part. You should not be able to get rid of your foundations easily, otherwise, who are you? You should be open to new ideas, and if your foundation is solid they will come in and sit easily with your own.

∞†∞
Think about it.

Put it in the front of your mind. Let your mind pick over it from all possible angles, probing and asking questions. Put all your resources to it.

∞†∞
If necessary, drop it.

If your conscious mind cannot find a solution let it drop from your mind. You may have brought it to the front of your mind a number of times. If you have done this and you end up thinking the same thing over and over, this is the time to drop it from your mind.

You will have had experience of finding solutions this way, suddenly appearing when you did not expect them to.

∞†∞
Nurture it.

The solutions that come to us from our subconscious can be like dreams. They are vivid and real and fantastic until you wake and let the questioning conscious mind get hold of them. Too soon they can be torn to shreds and tossed aside, often when the mind realises the effort involved to carry them through or just plain ridicules them. How to get over this is to nurture them, give them time.

Often the sub conscious idea you have will turn out to be even better than you thought, not worse. A solution you are using half-heartedly may turn out to be an opening to a whole new system once you see its full potential.

You may even find that you are trying to shake off an idea, you are trying to humiliate it and yourself but for some reason it cannot be got rid of. Eventually you will have to admit that you were wrong and that the idea is working very well. You will then notice how quickly things can develop from this point. Sometimes this can be the catalyst, not just for a greater acceptance of the one use of the new thing, but often you can be propelled forward to find numerous new applications for it.

You can help this process and prompt it by literally saying to yourself, 'What if it is better than I am thinking, not worse?' You can eventually use this principle when you first get a thought out of your subconscious to protect it in its first fragile early days. You will find it becomes obvious if it is not a good idea, but it needs protecting for a time.

You will obviously need to gain much experience before this can be possible.

∞‡∞
When a new route stares you in the face.

This is different to the situation were you are searching for a solution. This is when the situation comes to you. You will be on the edge of your knowledge and understanding. You will see the boundary before you and in your mind it will be a question of do you go forward or stay back. It is like stepping into the dark, a great void where you do not know what is going to happen. You might put yourself in danger, it might be a situation that does not go anywhere or it might be the creation of a whole new world.

You must press on and discover what happens. The best way is with a trusted training partner. Someone you can trust. Someone you can explain too, what you are trying to do. You can then try your discovers in more purposeful circumstances.

Sometimes these situations come to you in the middle of a difficult fight. You need to analyse as much as possible the cost and benefits of your more. You need to visualise in your mind the movement of your body and theirs.

∞‡∞
General.

As a new move is found and passed through the martial arts community it is like the discovery of a medical compound that works. It goes through stages of refinement and analysis to find the active ingredient that works. In martial arts terms the move becomes slicker, smoother, has less elements

and looks stylised. It becomes easier to teach, but also easier to find ways
to combat and defend against.

Some fighters become enamoured with this stylisation, trapped by it. If you
look at a champion fighter they do not fight like this. There is a sense that
they are somehow a little sloppy, that they are offering chances to their
opponent and an element of surprise that they have overcome their
opponent who may have looked better. What it is is that the loser was
more stylised, easier to understand while the champion's successful moves
are hidden in his overall movement and are more difficult to understand
and counteract.

15 THE FINAL WORD

When sportsmen retire, it is the locker room that they miss. The old soldier stories, the banter, the characters. Love the atmosphere in your club, the people and the camaraderie. Enrich your club with what you do and who you are. People should look at you and be thinking that your parents have done a good job.

ABOUT THE AUTHOR

As well as spending many years rolling around mats with sweaty people, I also enjoy football and fell running. Those hills are hard.

Born in Bury, Lancashire I am a business studies graduate from Thames Polytechnic, now gloriously renamed Greenwich University. After spending five years in marketing and sales I went into teaching mathematics in secondary schools.

Printed in Poland
by Amazon Fulfillment
Poland Sp. z o.o., Wrocław